PREFACE

What is "good ministry?" What does it look like? What calls it forth and nurtures it? What hinders it? Answers to these important and provocative questions were invited from a number of nationally known theological educators and pastors to stimulate discussion at a conference on Good Ministry in January 2002. These persons were asked to offer their answers in short papers for discussion at the conference. Convened by the Fund for Theological Education, conference participants represented theological schools that had received grants from Lilly Endowment Inc. for projects aimed at strengthening congregational leadership. At the conference, participants and authors engaged in lively conversation about the Good Ministry papers. Sparking the lively discussions was an opening plenary panel with presentations by three pastors who exemplify good ministry.

The Fund for Theological Education (FTE) and Pulpit & Pew: Research on Pastoral Leadership are pleased to make a selection of these Good Ministry papers and the three clergy panelists' presentations available for wider discussion and reflection on the meaning and practice of good ministry.

There are two obvious ways for using this resource. You can simply read these rich, provocative papers on Good Ministry on your own and profit from the insights. Better still, you might convene a group that will use these papers as the basis for group reflection—for example, in a theological faculty retreat, a seminary class, a clergy discussion group, a pastor-parish relations committee in a congregation, a Sunday school class, or a pastoral search committee, to mention just a few possibilities. In doing this, you might consider inviting members of your group to write their own descriptions of good ministry. You may also want to chose a moderator to "set the table" for a productive conversation, for example, establishing the time frame, setting the tone of collegial exchange, etc.

We highly commend both of these options—individual reading and group discussion. Our goal is to encourage you to use this resource as a model for structuring original thinking and strategic conversation about good ministry. To that end, we not only present the papers, but we've asked each writer to append several questions for further reflection and discussion.

The Fund for Theological Education (FTE) promotes excellence and diversity in pastoral ministry and theological scholarship. It aims to be a strong advocate for the profession of ministry and a resource about and for ministry. FTE coordinates several Lilly Endowment-sponsored grant programs for strengthening congregational leadership, including Programs to Enhance the Capacities of Theological Schools to Prepare Congregational Leadership. Individuals and grants from various U.S. foundations support the Fund's work. For a description of FTE programs, see the Web site, **www.thefund.org**.

Pulpit & Pew is a multifaceted study of pastoral leadership, Catholic and Protestant, being undertaken at Duke University's Divinity School with funding from Lilly Endowment. Its purpose is to provide credible research findings about pastoral leadership today and the changes impacting it. Three central sets of questions guide the research:

• What is the state of pastoral leadership at the new century's beginning, and what do current trends portend for the next generation?

• What is "good ministry?" Can we describe it? How does it come into being?

• What can be done to help "good ministry" to come into being more frequently, and how can it be nurtured and supported more directly?

More information about Pulpit & Pew and additional reports are available at the project Web site, **www.pulpitandpew.duke.edu**.

On behalf of FTE and Pulpit & Pew, we commend these reflections on good ministry to you.

Carol E.Lytch, Coordinator
Theological School Programs for Strengthening
Congregational Leadership
Fund for Theological Education
Louisville Presbyterian Theological Seminary

Jackson W. Carroll, Director
Pulpit & Pew: Research on Pastoral Leadership
Duke Divinity School

PART I
THREE PORTRAITS OF GOOD MINISTRY

1. Minute Fifty Four

Lillian Daniel[*]

I began my day at the intensive care unit at the hospital, searching for a room. I have entered the hospital under false pretenses, because nobody ever believes I am a minister.

Put aside the fact that I am not male and wearing a collar in Roman Catholic New Haven, I am not even accepted as a Protestant, because these days, we recruit fewer and fewer first-career clergy.

The way that trickles into my life is that whenever I show up at hospitals, I am judged too young. "You couldn't possibly be a minister," I am told, by people who say this as if they are the first people to honor me with their refreshing honesty. But of course being called "too young" does get, well…old.

So I have adopted the custom of entering hospitals without wearing my clergy badge, walking the floors with a certain sleepy confidence that I copy from the doctors who tend to be my age. Too young to pray at bedsides, apparently I am just the right age to wield a scalpel.

Without my clergy badge, I get in everywhere. It's *The Wizard of Oz.* Wake up, Lillian. You're not in Christendom anymore.

And now I find myself at the intensive-care bedside of one of the saints of our church, who has struggled with cerebral palsy since her childhood. Now, after a rich life, in old age she is slipping away from a world of pain.

Her words are slurred these days but her mind is sharp. Together, in the midst of beeping machines and anxious faces, we try to get the doctor's attention.

We ask him to change the policy of limiting visits to family members. She has no living family. But there are church members who have visited over the years, and now they want to visit one last time. Finally, the doctor understands.

"OK. It's like the church is her family," he mutters, making a note on her chart. Perhaps it is the same note that God made long ago in the book of cherished life.

Our conversation ends in her making a living will with this doctor. As I listen to these words being exchanged, I realize that in the Christian walk, we pay holy attention to one another, eavesdropping on moments and words that the world may not understand.

It takes a holy imagination to know that the living will in her medical chart is not the last word, but that in the beginning was the Word that has and will give her life.

Wondering if it is ever a good time to leave her bedside, I eavesdrop back through the centuries to Jesus' promise to his disciples in John 14:18, *I will not leave you orphaned.*

I love being a minister. Even when the ministry is hard, it's more fun than any other job I can imagine. Where else can you preach, teach, meet with a lead abatement specialist, and get arrested for civil disobedience all in the same week?

Where else can you be invited into the living rooms of new mothers and into the hospice rooms of the dying and find hope in both places? I do love being a minister. I love the agility it calls forth in me and the chaos that only Jesus could organize into a calling.

I should also say that I loved my theological training and the educational experience in general, from Bryn Mawr College, where they told us we weren't girls but women (who knew?), to Yale, where we read the texts so closely, to Hartford Seminary, where we read the congregations so intensely, and now a project at Duke Divinity School, where they read the ministry so passionately.

Lately I've had the chance to teach preaching and to participate with my teachers in shaping people like me in a wider Christian tradition that is greater than us all. When I think of how all of our callings come together, from church pews to seminary seats to pulpit chairs, I think of this.

There is a woman in my church who suffered a stroke, from which she is gradually recovering her ability to speak. But the last thing to come is our names.

Church people visit her, and she can speak to us in ways that indicate she knows exactly who we are and has known us for years, but she cannot speak anybody's name. Instead she pulls out the church photo directory.

[*] Lillian Daniel is the Senior Minister of the Church of the Redeemer, United Church of Christ, in New Haven, Conn.

When one of us from the church walks in, she waves that sacred directory at us, as if to say that she does not know our names, but she knows the way in which we are all related. She may have forgotten our names but she knows us as we truly are.

When I look back to the education of my generation, I realize that we spent a great deal of time on names. We wrestled with questions of language as if our lives depended upon it, drawing lines between ourselves based on our words and our names.

But in the life of my local church, a church that in the last five years has become more interracial and diverse in many ways, when the Holy Spirit is with us, we are forgiven if we forget one another's names. We're allowed to remember, instead, the ways in which we are related.

It's that sense of being related that takes me in my ministry to the places I do not want to go. Many of us enter the ministry thinking that we are entering a world of ideas, when really it is such an earthy calling. Nothing in my training could have prepared me, a person who once had the luxury of fainting at the sight of blood, for all that time in hospitals.

Nothing could have taught me how to pray through the beeps of machines and to hold hands around the work of wet washcloths and nurses aides. Nothing could have taught me how to sit by a bedside and pretend not to notice the strong smell of urine.

Nothing could have prepared me for how tiny and small the corporate lawyer looks in his hospital gown, of how people's faces seem to fold into blandness when they lie in a coma. Nothing could have prepared me for how terribly earthy the ministry is; how incarnational.

What prepared me for that was Jesus, and the trust that for some reason God chose to come to this world of pain in bodily form. Sometimes, my calling as a minister is to count the broken bodies in the world and call them God's.

Some of those broken bodies would be churches. It seems to me that the church I was trained in seminary to expect was some sort of cocky country club fortress that needed to be taken down a peg or two.

We, the new ministers, would come flying in like Underdog, armed with new hymnals, new language, and new ideas, inspired by professors who were still passionately processing their two years in the ministry fifteen years ago.

The church I was trained to expect was a church that needed fixing, not in its weakness, but in its hubris.

The church I was called to serve, as a minister, turned out to be a body broken in different ways. Sure, some of our congregations dress up in statistics that seem sleek. But the average seminarian will go out to serve a struggling church, perhaps a couple of struggling churches.

Having read about mega-churches she finds herself instead next door to the mega-church, wondering what she is doing wrong. Meanwhile, at the mega-church, they are wondering what they are doing wrong, as more members slip out than skip in.

As an associate minister, my first congregation was a thriving suburban church that presented a beautiful façade on the New England green but privately struggled to overcome the pedophilia charges against the last associate minister.

When I moved to my present congregation, they had an endowment, a gorgeous building, a wonderful reputation, and about twenty-five people worshipping on Sunday. These were not churches that needed to be taken down a peg or two.

In the last years, our church has grown enough to be a statistical success. But in our current fat years, I will still bristle at the slightest hint of condescension toward any church's life together, for in my mind, I see the faces of the people who worked so hard to see people sit in those pews in our lean years.

Some of our churches have been taken down so many pegs they feel the next step will be the ground, and so they snarl and hiss at change as if they are about to die. Because some of them are. But some of them are about to live.

In school, I was taught the tools of critique, and how to search out the weakness in the argument, even the signs of death and decay. But what about life?

Are we schooled in searching out the life? Can you be taught how to look for signs of grace? If there is a pastoral imagination, this must be at the heart of it.

I think of this later in my day, as I sit at my desk faced with an open Bible. Preparing to preach is both exhilarating and humbling. I love to preach and have grown used to it, and yet this moment before I start to write still sends an electric thrill through my soul.

The passage is Hebrews 11:1: *Now faith is the assurance of things hoped for, the conviction of things not seen.*

So much in the ministry is not seen, but hoped for. So much that we do rests tenderly in the heart of Jesus but may not be noticed here on earth. It still surprises me to find that my hip, postmodern life has already been described in the book of Hebrews.

Even though I grew up in the church, I did not grow up loving scripture. Like many in mainline Protestant traditions, I was raised in Sunday schools in which we got a lot of situational ethics. (Remember the lifeboat dilemma, in which you discuss what to do with the thirteenth person in the twelve person boat? I believe that was confirmation class for many of us…)

We had discussions about our feelings. ("I, like, have a, like, problem with the Apostles Creed…." "OK , we can hear you in that, Lillian…say more…") But the closest we got to Christology was "color in that ditto of the baby Jesus, and don't spill your juice."

Perhaps pastoral imagination is really Christian imagination, the ability to see eschatologically, to see with the eyes of the heart enlightened.

Like the proverbial football player who graduates without knowing how to read, we could sneak through our church's Christian education process as Biblical illiterates.

I discovered scripture as an adult, and, if I am honest, as a preacher. It's amazing that God can work with such broken vessels.

But because I came to this love late in life, I am convinced that all ministry is a teaching ministry. God would not have us leave our brains out on the sidewalk in front of the church doors. When I finish a sermon, what I want people to remember is the scripture.

If what they remember is only a story I told, I have failed as a preacher of the gospel, and become a tawdry after-dinner speaker who happens to be on the after-breakfast circuit. So just the act of preparing to preach is all about hope and imagining a transformation that can only be God's.

Perhaps pastoral imagination is really Christian imagination, the ability to see eschatologically, to see with the eyes of the heart enlightened. I think of my academic training in the close reading of a text and realize that I still do that, but the text is not simply the scripture or a theologian. The text is also the congregation.

My job in the preaching moment is to read our lives as a community and reflect it back through the lens of faith. To claim our broken bodies as God's.

And sometimes, when my ministry goes awry, or is not all it could be, I claim my own broken body as God's and try to learn.

I remember once I found myself in the place where a lot of broken bodies end up, locked into a State of Connecticut police paddy wagon. When I had pictured my own arrest for civil disobedience at our governor's office in support of some striking nursing home workers, I had imagined myself in the company of scores of other clergy. The workers, beaten down in their strike, returned to work to find they were locked out and replaced by temps who were paid by our tax dollars. If there's one thing the earthy call and hospital visits give you, it's a fierce respect for health care workers and a sense of shame at how our society treats them.

So hundreds of locked out, striking workers gathered in the capitol building and sang "Amazing Grace" as we were pulled away, but instead of scores of clergy, only four were arrested, and now I was alone in the paddy wagon.

In a moment of self-indulgent bitterness, I wondered how the church of Jesus could produce so many ministers willing to fall on their swords over issues of sexuality, but unwilling to notice the demonic gap between the rich and the poor.

My bitterness was the result of loneliness. I had not expected to be searched with rubber gloves, to have my things taken away, to lose the wallet snapshots of my grinning, toothless children, and to be kept alone for such a long time.

I was angry at myself. I had failed to warn my church members of my actions. Thinking I would be in a larger crowd, I had not prepared them to see me on the evening news. I could have done this better.

Now, I was analyzing my own leadership intensely. And alone in the paddy wagon, surrounded by trash, the smell of vomit, and so much self-examination, I wanted to go back to the minister I was before I thought about these things, who acted first and asked questions later, if at all.

I wanted to see less of myself.

As the door clanged shut, suddenly I could only see light through a tiny window that was barred. The one police officer caught my eye.

"This stuff is pretty inhumane, isn't it?" he said.

"I feel like an animal in a cage," I said.

"And you're getting the royal treatment."

"Thanks," I said.

"If it makes you feel any better," he added, "I spent two nights in one of those things with a bunch of drunks, back in the military. You don't even want to know. It was disgusting…"

Before the actual arrest, I had the romantic notion that I might pray in the paddy wagon, but this guy was talking my ear off, ruining the spiritual scenery with his real life.

"Why are you in this field, if you hate it so much?" I asked, perhaps wondering about my own future in my field.

"Just fell into it, I guess. After the military. So I retire in two years, and I'm young. But what I wanted to say to you was something else. What I wanted to say to you, was that back there, when you guys were singing 'Amazing Grace,' in the capitol building, I liked that. I liked the way your voices sounded when you sang those songs. So I wanted to let you know."

"Thanks, again," I said.

"You'll get out of here soon," he said.

"You too," I said. But all of a sudden, I could see it.

If there's a way of life and a way of death, they flip quickly. The holy imagination can paint a picture of a new life where there are no bars and chains. His story about our singing, our practice of the faith, allowed me to imagine once again a world in which no one is locked in, or locked out.

When we caught each other's eyes, through the little bars, we realized we were both thinking about the same thing: freedom. But we were not just thinking about it any more. Now, we could imagine it.

In the more ordinary moments of ministry, I remember that moment of imagination, and how as a church we worked through our differences of opinion about whether one's minister should be hauled off in hand-cuffs. That news clipping of my arrest went up on the bulletin board, and down again, up and down, until it became a running joke. But not every day in the church offers that kind of excitement.

I think back to the visit to the intensive care unit that morning and how unprepared I was for the scene God was unfolding. As carefully as I try to plan, as much attention as I give to the details, I never know what will happen in the ministry. I realize that actually, when you are following God's plan rather than your own, you're not meant to be an expert, just a person who can notice grace in earthy places.

Back at the church a few hours later, the Trustees are meeting. The Trustees are indeed the trusted ones, the lay leaders entrusted with managing the financial and physical resources of our New England Con-gregational church. We Congregationalists are fairly earthy ourselves.

We like to say that the members run the church, not some faraway hierarchy. Of course when the members run the church, that probably doesn't leave quite enough room for Jesus.

At this meeting, I am thinking about giving a talk at the forum of the Fund for Theological Education, about the lofty ideas about theological education I will hear over those days. I am tuning in and out as the Trustees discuss another of their duties: they must take their twice-yearly turn preparing and serving the meal at the homeless shelter.

Is the discussion about hospitality as a practice of the faith and the theology behind it? Is the conversation about how we could do more to solve the problems of homelessness as a systemic evil, instead of simply serving food? Alas, no. The heated discussion is about the correct recipe for chili mac, that strange American casserole that dares to cross macaroni and cheese with canned chili and call it food.

As I consider the nature of the pastoral imagination, I sit through a forty-five minute discussion about chili mac. Do you get the large cans of chili or the small ones? Does anyone have a membership to a discount warehouse? And then there is the particularly contentious issue: should we buy grated cheese or grate it ourselves?

Someone remembers that they do not have a cheese grater at the shelter. Should we buy one or just spend extra on the grated cheese? Let's do a cost comparison, someone suggests, whipping out the calculator. This is the board of Trustees after all.

Just as we are nearing a decision, a new board member asks, "Why do we always make chili mac? The last time, the people said they were tired of it. Besides, some of the homeless are vegetarians."

I know what's coming next and I cringe…

"How can you be homeless and be vegetarian?" a veteran inevitably asks.

The younger members of the board glare at him.

Now it's been fifty minutes. On chili mac. This moment is eternity. I am losing my religion. I have lost my eschatology. Fifty-one minutes.

I find myself dreaming of the past. I remember feeling a call to preach having never even once laid eyes on a woman minister until I set off for Divinity School, basically on a hunch, that I might find one.

I think back to the papers I wrote, staying up all night on fire for God and the theology of one person or another. Was my first inkling of the pastoral imagination my own call to the ministry?

I think of the prayers I said earlier that day at the hospital bedside and wonder if the woman I prayed with is even still in this world.

"Can I go back to an earlier point?" the clerk of the Trustees asks. "Did you decide on the grated cheddar cheese or to purchase a cheese grater? I need to get this right for the minutes."

For this I spent three years in graduate school.

Sometimes, it takes pastoral imagination just to remember a call, to imagine one, not in the sense that the call is an illusion created by us, but to imagine it as to see what we do not know, to see the possibilities God has for us.

To see God's possibilities even in the midst of grated cheese or broken bodies, because in the end, they are not so different. They both point to the fragility of life, the desperate delicacy with which we try to live with order, balance, and meaning in a chaotic world.

When I think of the pastoral imagination, I consider that we can be prepared by one another for what is really out there, but it is God who prepares us for what might be out there.

Christ crucified and resurrected prepares us to find majesty in the ordinary, mystery in the concrete, love in the midst of feuding, a ministry of tending to the details in the midst of grated cheese.

"I'd hate to be homeless, on a night like this," one of the Trustees says, and for a moment the clerk puts down his pen, the calculator is pushed aside, and everyone is silent, and I feel as if I hear God's pen making a scratchy note in the book of our cherished lives.

And then the meeting goes on, to the space requests and the broken window panes, but there was that moment when we were all quiet, and we could hear each other breathe, and we could hear who had a cold, and who was a runner, and who was choked up.

And that was the moment that was really eternity.

And it carried us soaring.

Into minute fifty four.

2. TURNAROUND AT OLD ST. PATRICK'S CHURCH

Fr. Jack Wall*

One of the characteristics of good leadership is the capacity of the leader to connect a group's historic past and ideals to new dreams for the group's future. John F. Kennedy did this with great effectiveness as he proposed his vision of a New Frontier at Boston's Faneuil Hall, a crucial site for our nation's early history. Similarly, Dr. Martin Luther King Jr. chose the Lincoln Memorial as the place where he proposed his vision of a new America, one where whites and blacks would sit together at the same table. In both cases, they brought historic values and ideals together as they put forward a vision for the future.

When I was assigned to Old St. Patrick's Church in Chicago, I came to a parish that was essentially dead, or quite nearly so. Yet, it was a parish that had an important past. It has been a place of hospitality, one in which waves of immigrants had found a welcome, a place where they were able to connect the faith and memories that they had brought with them to their experiences in a new land. I took this important parish heritage and used it as part of the basis for a new vision that would give new life to the parish.

Shaped not only by this heritage, but by the Second Vatican Council's understanding of ministry as belonging to the whole people of God and a belief that Christ is manifest through the ministry of God's people, my vision for Old St. Patrick's was as a mission-centered rather than a member-centered church. The central question that I and the lay leaders began to ask each other was not, "What do you need?" but "What is our mission?" This new vision, with roots in the parish's past, was especially focused in two areas: (1) A ministry to young adults who were mainly outside the congregation. As they were attracted to the church's ministries, they also often brought their parents. (2) Ministry in public life, especially programs that focused on the intersection of faith and work.

Old St. Patrick's is not an ideological church but a pastoral one. There is a sense of inclusiveness that

welcomes people of differing ideologies. The operative theology of the parish is a focus on the church as an "event," one in which the experience of Christ's presence is central. To be sure, the church is also an institution, but the primary concern is to make experience central and not to get bogged down in institutional maintenance.

With this as the vision that energizes the parish, three practices have become central: First is the practice of hospitality—welcoming strangers as gifts to be celebrated—much as the church did for new immigrants in the past. As the parish's Web site expresses it, "Fr. Jack Wall often speaks of hospitality as being a primary virtue of Christianity, exemplified by such a simple act as when Abraham and Sarah welcomed the stranger. One way Old St. Pat's continues this tradition is by welcoming those who have dreams of creating something life-giving" (**www.oldstpats.org**). Second, the parish emphasizes that every member is called to ministry and works to help each member gain the resources needed to exercise her or his ministry. Third, the parish has a focus on the public arena, especially as individual members live out their vocations in this arena, and finding many ways to emphasize the intersection between faith and work.

In these ways, a dying church has been helped to gain a new vision for itself that built on its heritage as a place of welcome to immigrants. In doing so, it has become once again, a place of vital ministry and mission in the city.

* Summary notes from a presentation by Fr. Jack Wall, Pastor of Old St. Patrick's Church, Chicago, Ill., to the Forum on Good Ministry, Indianapolis, Ind., January 8-9, 2002. (The summary has been approved by Fr. Wall.)

3. Sustained by Spiritual Friendships in the Gaps

Felicia Y. Thomas*

I entered the Master of Divinity program at Union Theological Seminary in New York with a clear and urgent sense of vocation: pastoral ministry. I received a long-awaited pastoral call to serve a church in my Baptist denomination. I resigned after six years on an Easter Sunday. At that point I was convinced that I would never serve a congregation in pastoral ministry again.

The decision to leave was the most painful decision of my life—more gut wrenching and heartbreaking than the untimely death of my youngest brother at age seventeen. I left with a profound sense that it was time for me to go. It became clearer and clearer to me that our future health—that of the congregation and myself—required a radically different way of relating as pastor and people together. I spent years bridging the chasms between young and old, between long-standing and new-coming, between those celebrating the past and those trying to embrace the future. Those years took a toll on me and on my family. I realized that I was neither Abraham nor Sarah. I was not willing or able to imagine building a ministry on the wreckage of my family. Somehow that just did not square with my conviction about the abundant life that Christ promised believers. Prayerfully, tearfully, and painfully, I parted. I knew how Jochebed must have felt when she laid her precious, beautiful baby in a handmade ark and launched it on the Nile.

Seasoned pastors say that pastoral ministry is like marriage, and in some ways it is. I find pastoral ministry to be more like mothering. It was the experience of birthing and raising my two young sons, while concurrently serving as pastor to a congregation, that makes the parallel for me. Both teach me how to love unconditionally, to serve with humility, to delight in the ordinary, and ultimately to let go. During that final Holy Week, I sobbed in agony daily and begged God to send someone else to love and nurture the congregation that I could no longer hold secure.

My seminary education did not include teaching about the gaps in ministry—the spaces between discerning a pastoral vocation and finding a place where it can flourish—and how to survive them. During the gaps that represented crisis points in my ministry, I had to learn how to be sustained. I was nourished, healed, and encouraged by deep, rich spiritual friendships of incredible tenacity and fidelity.

In the gap I experienced after leaving the congregation I served for six years, for example, I was invited to participate in a Pastor's Working Group for dialogue and interaction with a set of pastors gathered from different parts of the country. I made new friends with colleagues I never would have known otherwise, Catholic and Protestant, black and white, male and female. For two days, every six to eight weeks, over the course of sixteen months, we read, wrote, reflected, talked, questioned, challenged, worshipped, dined, and were nourished by one another. We explored ideas, situations, and practices of pastoral ministry. Who knew that there might be such a thing as "a pastoral imagination?" We embarked on a spiritual quest together and discovered the existence of vast pastoral intelligence and wisdom within one another and within our own selves.

I have been able to return to the pastorate where I currently serve in the East Village of New York City. The congregation is supported in its ministry by a staff of colleagues—friends in ministry—of which I am privileged to be a part. We are called "ministry associates"—clergy and lay, senior, middler, and junior in experience. We are all friends. We talk theology, ethics, biblical criticism, church history, congregational studies, sexuality, psychology, literature, and pop culture. We read and swap books. We collaborate on projects and programs. Friendship keeps us accountable and makes the work joyful.

When I was a little girl, my pastor often admonished us with the words, "if you want to have friends, you must show yourself friendly." Developing and maintaining the kinds of spiritual friendships that help to sustain life and ministry over the long haul is mostly a matter of being open and friendly, of listening and sharing, of praying and seeking, of dining and dancing, of laughing and crying together. As in any mean-

---

* Felicia Y. Thomas is Minister for Congregational Life, Middle Collegiate Church, New York, N.Y.

ingful relationship there is intimacy, authenticity, and integrity. Spiritual friendships play a vital role in good ministry, both for congregations and the pastors who serve them.

I come out of a black church tradition in which Jesus is viewed as the ultimate friend. I grew up singing lots of songs about the friendship of Christ: "What a Friend We Have in Jesus;" "Jesus is My Only Friend;" "He is My Best Friend;" and this favorite gospel song, "That Kind of Friend."

THAT KIND OF FRIEND

If you ever need a friend
that sticks closer than any (other),

I'd recommend Jesus
because He is THAT kind of friend.

He won't ever—he'll never forsake you,

Even though he knows
everything there is to know about you.

I'd recommend Jesus
because He is THAT kind of friend.

He'll walk right in front of you to always protect you.

So the devil can't do you no harm.

He is faithful everyday to help you along the way.

He is THAT kind of friend.

Over the years I have learned that Christ is a great friend. Still, I must confess my joy and gratitude that Christ's friendship has been embodied throughout my life and ministry in relationship with other human pilgrims. I am glad that Jesus is not my only friend.

PART II
PERSPECTIVES ON GOOD MINISTRY

4. INGREDIENTS OF GOOD AND FAITHFUL MINISTRY

Thomas G. Long*

In *Open Secrets: A Spiritual Journey through a Country Church*[1], Richard Lischer's finely crafted book about his early years as a Lutheran pastor in the farm community of Cana, Illinois, he writes, "In Cana we baptized our babies, celebrated marriages, wept over the dead, and received Holy Communion, all by the light of our best window."

What Lischer calls "our best window" was a stained glass depiction of no less than the doctrine of the Trinity, set high into the east wall of the sanctuary above the altar. Though it was a piece of "ecclesiastical boilerplate" from a studio in Chicago, it was nonetheless impressive both for its rich colors and its sturdy insistence on classical theology. A large central triangle, labeled DEUS, was surrounded by three smaller triangles, marked respectively PATER, FILIUS, and SPIRITUS SANCTUS. Each smaller triangle was connected to the larger DEUS triangle by a little highway marked EST, and each smaller triangle was connected to the other small triangles by highways marked NON EST. "Our window's geometric design," observes Lischer, "seemed to say, 'Any questions?'"

Thinking about the relationships between this window, his ministry, and the life of his congregation, Lischer observes,

> We believed that there was a correspondence between the God who was diagramed in that window and our stories of friendship and neighborliness. If we could have fully taken into our community the name Trinity, we would have needed no further revelations and no more religion, for the life of God would have become our life.

An aerial photographer once remarked that from the air you can see paths, like the canals on Mars, that crisscross pastures and fields among the farms where neighbors have trudged for generations, just to visit or help one another in times of need. These, too, are the highways among *Pater, Filius,* and *Spiritus Sanctus* grooved into human relationships. The word "religion" comes from the same root as "ligaments." These are the ties that bind.

I want to take this image of the complex and finally mysterious Trinity window shining down on a pastor and on his little congregation doing their work of prayer and neighborly service and expand upon it a bit, because it seems to me to suggest several of the ingredients of good and faithful ministry:

1. Faithful ministry is primarily leadership that seeks to deepen the correspondence between the life of a faith community and what God is doing in and for the world.

Just as Lischer saw the pattern and paths of the mystery of the Trinity "grooved into human relationships," so faithful ministry seeks to enable the life of a faith community to conform to the shape of God's life in the world. This means exerting leadership in two directions. First, faithful ministers help establish and support practices that seek to discover the mystery of God-with-us (such as prayer, the study of scripture, meditation, honest preaching, reflection on religious experience and the social realities), and, second, they encourage an active and ongoing rethinking of how the community's life can and should respond to these discoveries.

Take worship leadership as an example. Faithful ministry would neither demand lockstep obedience to a prayer book nor would it encourage a congregation to frame its liturgical life as a set of solutions for a series of pragmatic problems ("Geez, how can we get more young people involved in worship?" or "What are we going to do about these people who want a praise band?"). Rather, it would begin by seeking to know of the phenomenon of worship itself, of what happens when human beings fall down in adoration before the *mysterium tremendum,* and then proceed by asking after the marvelous variety of liturgical expressions, sequences, and patterns that radiate from and conform to the shape of that essential encounter. The same quest for congruence to the patterns of God's interaction with the world would apply to other areas of the community's life and mission, such as education, fellowship, and works of justice.

---

* Thomas Long is Bandy Professor of Preaching, Candler School of Theology, Emory University, Atlanta, Ga.

[1] All quotations from Lischer are from "Our Best Window," chapter 8 in Richard Lischer, *Open Secrets: A Spiritual Journey through a Country Church* (New York: Doubleday, 2001), 80-87.

2. Faithful ministry is responsive to and expressive of a rich, living, and developing theological tradition.

While it is true that faithful ministry is certainly not a matter of mere repetition or imitation, it does grow out of a profound awareness that every minister is a temporary occupant of a venerable office grounded in a rich theological heritage and disciplined by practices honed against the stones of experience and wisdom. In short, faithful ministers convey in everything they do the calm assurance that we have been this way before and that we are not making this all up. "We sensed," said Lischer, "that our window stood as a witness against the religion 'of our own sweet invention' as [Flannery] O'Connor put it...."

This is an especially important affirmation in a culture where the emphasis often falls on personal charisma and magnetism in leaders. Much that passes for exciting ministry is, in the end, self-referential, pointing only to the minister's cleverness and charm. To exercise faithful ministry is to assume a role much like that of a dynamic conductor guiding an orchestra and chorus through Vivaldi's *Gloria*. Through a combination of energy, personality, persuasion, venturesomeness, knowledge, and skill, the conductor summons the best gifts of the musicians, and at the end of the evening the audience knows that, because of the conductor's abilities and efforts, they did not receive the conductor but the *Gloria*.

3. Faithful ministry involves the alert and poetic rethinking of this theological tradition, allowing the highway between creed and community religious practice to be well-traveled in both directions.

Having made the point that faithful ministry is responsive to a rich theological tradition, it must now be said that no living tradition is static and that good ministry takes place where the rhythmic tide of the deep washes across the changing shoreline of the culture. Thus, faithful ministry requires a vigilant imagination, a nimble willingness to see the shifting patterns in the tidal basins and to rethink how the ancient symbols and metaphors freshly engage and are engaged by new circumstances. When Lischer sees the links between the inner logic of the Trinity and the well-trod paths connecting neighbors across Illinois cornfields, he has made the sort of imaginative connection between tradition and circumstance that is the product of the vision needed for effective ministry.

This expression of faithful ministry takes place in a risky middle ground between mechanical and formulaic thinking (The Bible says...the Discipline commands...the Creed insists) on the one side and rootless innovation on the other. This rather involves the kind of ironic theological imagination we find in Isaiah 43:18-19. After having powerfully evoked the memory of the Exodus, the prophet paradoxically says:

> *Do not remember the former things, or consider the things of old.*
>
> *I am about to do a new thing; now it springs forth, do you not perceive it?*
>
> *I will make a way in the wilderness and rivers in the desert.*

Here we see the ancient images both honored and reversed, yielding both continuity and discontinuity. The God who once produced "a way in the sea" now makes a "way in the wilderness," and the God who carved a dry path in the waters now makes "rivers in the desert." Faithful ministry is fueled by this ironic theological imagination, an awareness that God does what God has always done but in every new, unexpected, and surprising ways.

One consequence of this poetic theological imagination is the vigorous interaction of creed and practice. For example, the ancient command to show hospitality to the stranger comes toward the present community with ever fresh urgency and force, but that concept, forged in a village mentality and an honor shame society, must itself be influenced and modified by its placement in a global economy and a cybernetically linked world.

4. Faithful ministry is in, of, and for a particular community of people, but this ministry also must risk loneliness for the sake of this community.

Faithful ministry does not operate in isolation from a community of practicing believers. Indeed, ministry can be judged faithful to the extent that it is absorbed into the life of that community, nourishes the life of that community, directs attention away from itself so that it is finally seen not as an example of "good ministry," but as empowerment for faithful community practices. Thus good ministry is marked by gifts of an alertness to the other, the ability to build *koinonia*, and the celebration of the multiplicity of ministries within the one body (which, on tough days, means the ability to tolerate difficult people!).

However the paradox is that good ministry, precisely in order to equip the community of faith, must often have the courage to stand apart (sometimes even over against) the very community it seeks to serve. To bring in Lischer's image, good ministry stands in the middle ground between the pews and the mysterious "best window." Ministry is both priestly, turning toward the window on behalf of the people, and prophetic, turning toward the people to speak, however haltingly, the claims of the Mystery.

In his book *The Seduction of the Spirit*[2], theologian Harvey Cox described the small town Baptist church of his childhood in Malvern, Pennsylvania. He remembered the ministers who came and went every few years, observing that the minister was

> *... never completely at home in Malvern. ...He was always something of an outsider, without cousins and uncles in town. He was in, but not of, our world, to paraphrase St. Paul. His coming and going reminded me of that vast larger cosmos in which little Malvern was located. The preacher, even if he stayed five years, was always to some extent a stranger in a strange land. Maybe that gave him a little of the aura of transcendence or at least of the "otherness" the representative of God must always signify, whether he likes it or not.*

Good ministers have a simultaneous presence and absence, a familiarity and an unfamiliarity, an availability and a willingness to symbolize the untamable mystery without confusing that mystery with their own identity. Their energies are poured fully into the community's life, but they are not, to use another of Lischer's wonderful phrases, "a quivering mass of availability."

For Reflection:

1. How can good ministry serve and be guided by a faith tradition without being closed to new experiences and ideas?

2. Can you think of any examples of acts of ministry that fall in what the paper calls "a risky middle ground between mechanical and formulaic thinking," that is ministry that shows continuity with the past but responds creatively to the present challenges?

3. Do you agree with the paper that good ministry risks loneliness for the sake of community? Why or why not? Are there ways in which loneliness in ministry can be unhealthy, too?

[2] Harvey Cox, *The Seduction of the Spirit: The Use and Misuse of People's Religion* (New York: Simon and Schuster, 1973), 44.

5. RE-PRESENTING THE GRACE OF GOD IN CHRIST

Dorothy C. Bass*

The primary calling of every Christian is the same: to respond in trust and gratitude to the grace of God in Christ. This calling draws those who receive it into a way of life that embodies this response through love for and service to God and neighbor. Christian ministry occurs within and on behalf of such a way of life—a way that is truly life-giving not only for the church but also for the world. In this sense, good ministry belongs to every Christian individual and community.

The special vocation of those who are also called to *lead* Christian congregations is to draw the community's attention, again and again, to the grace of God in Christ that is at the heart of its way of life and, indeed, at the heart of the world itself. They are "ministers of Word and Sacrament"—ad-ministering those gifts wherein God's grace is believed to be most normatively, publicly, and specifically re-presented. Those responsible for Word and Sacrament serve the church's larger ministry best when they focus their energies and intelligence on offering these gifts to the people with vividness, clarity, honesty, and urgency.

Doing so in the midst of the rapidly changing and diverse culture of contemporary North America requires both deep historical and theological knowledge of Word and Sacrament and the capacity to engage in supple, sensitive, and imaginative ways with particular contexts of proclamation and celebration. The result is a tension that becomes, in the voice and hands of a skilful minister, a creative tension, as the specific stuff of a specific assembly is woven into the redemptive story of God. Those present may glimpse themselves and their world as new creation.[1]

Perhaps I can better explain what I mean by relating one instance of what I consider to be good ministry of this sort—even though it is an instance that contains no "real" sermon and no water, bread, or wine.[2] This re-presentation of Word and Sacrament took place at the end of a three-day meeting at which seventeen adults and seventeen teenagers laid plans for a book about the practices of the Christian life. On the whole, the meeting had been energizing and successful, though we had just run into some rough spots during the final early-morning session for the adults. If we had not committed ourselves to worshiping together before heading home, we might have kept on meeting for another hour. But now the younger folks were gathering; it was time to stop arguing and start singing.

As the meeting's host, I had asked Susan Briehl, an ELCA pastor, to lead this small, diverse assembly in its closing worship. Because it was Sunday and because important relationships were beginning to form within this group, Susan and I had wished that this worship might include Eucharist. Given the present limits of ecumenism, however, as well as our sense that the pieties of some in our group were less explicitly sacramental than our own, we had agreed that we would not share bread and wine that morning.

In spite of this limitation, the worship service gathered up the fragments of this group's experience, helped us to offer our life together to God in thanksgiving and supplication, clothed our experience (and us) in the language of the Gospel, and helped us to look with hope toward our future as a group and as members of humankind. We sang "Vamos todos," a rousing song in English and Spanish about gathering at God's banquet feast. Susan and her daughters read a children's book about a Great Table where everyone is welcome. We passed the peace.

The Scripture lesson was John 6:1-14 (the feeding of the five thousand). For the adults, this was a return to the text used in opening devotions at our first meeting,

---

* Dorothy Bass is Director of the Valparaiso Project on the Education and Formation of People in Faith, Valparaiso University, Valparaiso Ind.

[1] Miroslav Volf recently summarized the "barebones formal injunction of the gospel" as this: "Receive yourselves and your world as new creation." In "Theology for a Way of Life," in *Practicing Theology; Beliefs and Practices in Christian Life* (Eerdmans, 2002), p. 254.

[2] In his remarkable discussion of the meaning of Eucharist, David Ford suggests that the absence of a final meal in the Gospel of John constitutes a protest against "liturgical fundamentalism." See his *Self and Salvation* (Cambridge University Press, 1999), pp. 157-162.

five months earlier. At that time, Susan had pointed out that in John's gospel it is a young person who offers to share loaves and fishes with the crowd and led us in wondering what gifts our young colleagues would bring to our book. This time, she asked us to think about Jesus as one who eats with us and also with our future readers. She offered some reflections on Jesus at table and helped us to envision Jesus at the tables where we had eaten during the past three days. What stories did we know about Jesus eating with his friends? What stories could we tell about how Jesus had been present at our tables during the past three days? Where did we see Jesus eating with other young people, especially those in need? Soon many stories were being woven together. Some addressed hurtful divisions within our own group, some expressed longing for the well-being of teens all over the world. Some were funny. Susan initiated, guided, and closed the reflections, but many others also spoke.

Helping people to perceive the Living Word in the midst of very specific circumstances is the most important thing a minister does.

And then she brought forth stones, which some of the teenagers had harvested from a creek bed earlier that morning and painted with words like "forgiveness" and "managing our stuff" and "taking time" and "being friends"—the titles of the book chapters we were preparing to write. Each worshiper was to take one stone home and pray for the adult and teen who were writing about that practice. Somehow these stones, heavy and warm in our hands, seemed like bread.

Although no physical bread and wine were present, Susan found a way to invite everyone to a shared table where Christ is both host and feast. She encouraged the rest of us to share our gifts through music, words, and touch. She showed us how our tangible, incomplete activities in this specific time and place were part of God's activity in the world through the ages. She sent us out with a task that was both very specific and an emblem of the whole life of faith. And she made us (at least those of us from liturgical traditions who long for real bread and wine each Sunday) aware of our yearning for a time when divisions of many kinds will be no more.

Helping people to perceive the Living Word in the midst of very specific circumstances is the most important thing a minister does. Most frequently (and indispensably) this happens as he or she leads the gathered assembly in worship. The minister portrayed here knows that making God's gifts of Word and Sacrament available to *this* community in *this* time and place is her chief calling. She takes time and care to *craft* worship that leads to this result. This is not simply or even primarily a churchy-liturgical matter, for this craft depends on her continual gleaning from daily life of fresh images and insights that disclose the challenging grace Word and Sacrament can present to these particular people. All weekend long, she had been observing our meeting through the lens of John 6, listening for the rumblings of our hunger and watching closely as we grew into newfound table companionship. Good ministry thus depends on the minister's alertness to the voice of the Living Word as she engages in the daily life of a specific body of people, in ongoing study (her own and that of the group), and in daily awareness of the suffering and joy of the larger human family.

Good ministry also invites others into ministry. Through careful preparation, this minister made liturgy the work of the people. She invited participation during the service itself, drawing out the gifts and involvement of the assembly. It is worth noting that this was effective because so many of the members of this assembly *know* the stories that enabled them to participate fully. A pastoral commitment to strengthen the competence of the whole church—the stories folks know, the songs they sing, the gestures they make—would be an important component of good ministry of the sort described here. Also crucial is the assumption throughout—often made explicit—that the gifts of this people will bear fruit in the world as a result of this strengthening through Word and Sacrament. In sum, well-crafted, Christ-centered worship both gathers in our experience in the world and sends us out to love and serve God and one another.

In this example, we see a good minister exercising biblical imagination and being attentive to the dynamics of grace and sin in the everyday lives of specific people. These qualities also allow her to bring the images and insights of Word and Sacrament to ordinary weekday conversation and pastoral work—matters of great import in the life of a congregation. I have observed other ministers doing this brilliantly in the midst of running a board meeting, pitching a stewardship goal, visiting a bereaved family, and doing other essential ministerial tasks. For Susan and the others I know best, my perception is that worship is prior to and a condition for good ministry within these tasks, rather than the other way around. The quality of a minister's attention to the central act of the Christian life can order priorities, renew a call, and refresh theological convictions on a frequent and regular basis.

Let us return now to my opening image of the Christian calling into a way of life that embodies our response to the grace of God in Christ. "Worship is the point of concentration at which the whole of the Christian life comes to ritual focus," says the theologian Geoffrey Wainwright.[3] Worship orients us to the mysterious, awesome presence of the Triune God, from whom and toward whom all our living flows—not just our in-church living, but also the living we do at home and at work, the living we do as citizens, neighbors, children, parents, or friends. The focus that worship brings allows Christians to see the world in distinctive ways that a good minister can elucidate over the course of many weeks of preaching, presiding, teaching, conversing, and governing. This focus hones in on human needs and asks how we are created and what constitutes our true flourishing, rather than allowing consumer culture to define human needs. This focus allows us to recognize neighbors and companions where once there were strangers and ushers us into a way of life lived in relationship to others, face-to-face and across generations and continents and within a great communion of saints. This focus sees life where others see only death, allowing us to greet loss and failure without despair. I recently heard a good minister say how important it is to provide deep background in matters such as these, sometimes subtly and over the period of many years, so that when crisis comes, as it will, people will be ready to respond with courage and hope.

As I have pondered this question—"What is good ministry?"—I have had in mind the faces of people in my own congregation who lean forward in silent expectancy as each Sunday's sermon begins, hoping *this* time to receive the Living Word. I have pictured the parents who bring their babies to the font and the people of all ages who come forward to receive the Bread of Life. Good ministry offers to all of these the Real Thing, the Sacraments by which we are received into the Life of God, the Word that knows the difference between Life and Death.

FOR REFLECTION

1. The author writes that every Christian is called "to respond in trust and gratitude to the grace of God in Christ" through "love for and service to God and neighbor." Our calling or vocation, she says, is to "a way of life" that is "life-giving for the church and the world." In light of this definition, reflect on your own faith community's ministry. What specific realities currently shape it? How have these realities changed in the last decade? What changes do you foresee unfolding in the future? Are there specific circumstances and concrete realities that your congregation is ignoring or fleeing from as it plans its ministry and lives its life in gratitude to God and in response to the needs of neighbors, both nearby and around the world? After you have reflected on each of these questions, consider all these questions as a whole. Are questions like these primarily meant for the called and ordained ministers of congregations, or are they meant for all Christians? In fact, what members of your community give careful and consistent attention to the ministry of your congregation and its members?

2. Consider the relationship between the calling every Christian shares and the additional calling—what the author calls the "special vocation"—of those who lead Christian congregations as ministers of Word and Sacrament. Does the ordination of a few Christians diminish the ministry of the majority who are not ordained? How should ordained ministers understand the relationship between the vocation they share with other Christians and the special vocation to which they've also been called?

3. When have you perceived the Living Word in the midst of the "very specific circumstances" of your life or the life of your faith and community? How have you experienced, or how do you imagine, a minister helping you or your faith community to perceive the Living Word?

4. Do you agree that corporate "worship is prior to and a condition for good ministry"? If so, how does your congregation's use of its resources—such as money, time, imagination, and energy, including the time, gifts, and imagination of your minister—reflect the centrality of worship?

5. What do you think the people in your congregation long for as they gather to worship?

[3] *Doxology* (Oxford University Press, 1980), p. 8.

6. EMBODIMENT

Evelyn L. Parker*

When I consider the meaning of *good ministry* I think of a person rather than an abstract idea. I think of someone who embodies *good ministry/good service*, someone that holds within her flesh, bones, and sinew the memory of honor and shame, joy and sorrow, pleasure and pain, and justice and injustice. The body-self holds together the polarities of our experiences as well as unifies divine and human nature.[1] As such, the body-self becomes incarnate in God through the seamless divinity and humanity of Jesus of Nazareth.

Likewise, the body-self becomes like Jesus the sacrificial lamb laying down his life for the whole human community, surrendering his body to mutilation and death for the life of humankind. When Jesus Christ told his disciples to love one another he followed this commandment with a supporting declarative statement: "No one has greater love than this, to lay down one's life for one's friends" (John 15:13 NRSV). Jesus' words to his disciples foreshadowed the ultimate body-self experience as an act of service to humankind, his crucifixion. Jesus redeemed humankind with his body through the crown of thorns, the nails in his hands and feet, his thirst for water and the piercing of his side. The sacrificial act of Jesus' body illumines the centrality of embodiment to *good ministry*. His life and work are the ultimate model of *good ministry* and exemplify ministry as embodiment. Thus, *good ministry* is the body-self who incarnates the unity of the human and the divine Jesus, as well as one whose experiences compel a "radical commitment to lay down one's own life in the service of others."[2]

Mrs. Fannie Lou Hamer is a contemporary example of one who embodied *good ministry*. She was a noted activist during the Civil Rights Movement from the state of Mississippi. An exemplar of Christian convictions, organizer, lay preacher, inspirational singer, mother, and wife, Mrs. Hamer committed herself to the struggle for freedom and justice for people of color and the poor from the early 1950s until her death in 1977. Her life of service to the people of her community and to her country brought her center stage to many events including the 1964 Mississippi Freedom Summer Project, the 1964 and 1968 Democratic National Conventions, the 1969 founding of the Freedom Farm Project for the poor, both black and white, of Sunflower County, and the 1971 founding of the National Women's Political Caucus. The legendary phase of her life began in August of 1962 when she volunteered with seventeen other residents of Sunflower County to become registered voters. This first of several failed attempts to register to vote coupled with jeering angry white citizens and police harassment revealed Mrs. Hamer's gifts for public service, particularly through her gift of song. When it seemed the group would not return home safely after the police had stopped their bus and taken their driver, Mrs. Hamer calmed many of the riders on the bus while leading them in the singing of "Down by the Riverside," "Ain't Gonna Let Nobody Turn Me Around," and "This Little Light of Mine." Two thematic and interrelated practices in her ministry are instructive for understanding *good ministry*. These are the practice of prophetic public presence and the practice of the beloved community.

I will focus on the practice of prophetic public presence, or her ability to speak words of challenge and hope to political and religious powers in the public arena as well as grassroots people and motivate all to action. This is what Cornel West defines as a prophetic Afro-American Christian with the ability to "negate what is and transform prevailing realities against the backdrop of the present historical limits . . . thinking with the sobriety of tragedy, the struggle for freedom, and the spirit of hope."[3]

---

* Evelyn Parker is Assistant Professor of Christian Education, Perkins School of Theology, Southern Methodist University, Dallas, Tex.

[1] Anne Bathurst Gilson, "Embodiment" and "Incarnation" in Letty M. Russell and J. Shannon Clarkson (editors) *Dictionary of Feminist Theologies*, (Louisville, Kentucky: Westminster John Knox Press), p. 82 and 151.

[2] Henri Nouwen, *Creative Ministry* (New York: Image Books), p. 114.

[3] Cornel West, *Prophesy Deliverance! An Afro-American Revolutionary Christianity*, (Philadelphia: The Westminster Press), pp. 19-20.

At the heart of her prophetic public presence is the power of her voice. Her "stump-speaking style" and soul-stirring singing could calm fears, inspire commitment, and motivate action among civil rights workers.[4] "This Little Light of Mine" was the favorite song of Mrs. Hamer. Whether in jail, a mass meeting or during a civil rights march, she often sang this song to inspire others to persevere in the struggle for freedom.

> *This little light of mine, I'm gonna let it shine,*
> *Oh, this little light of mine, I'm gonna let it shine.*
> *This little light of mine, I'm gonna let it shine,*
> *Let it shine, let it shine, let it shine.*[5]

In an interview with Dale Gronemeier during the summer of 1964 she said:

> *This same song goes back to the fifth chapter of Matthew, which is the Beatitudes of the Bible when he says a city that sets on a hill cannot be hid. Let your light shine so shine that men [sic] would see your good works and glorify the father which is in heaven. I think singing is very important. It brings out the soul.*[6]

The power of her voice, its testimonies, preaching and singing, remains stamped in the minds of many people across the United States.

Mrs. Hamer's favorite song and the scripture reference that she uses to interpret its meaning provide the rubric for understanding her embodiment of *good ministry*. She understood herself as "…the light of the world" shining before others, so that they may see her good works and give glory to God (Matthew 5:14 NRSV). This epistemological and ontological self-declaration of Mrs. Hamer reveals her incarnate and her sacrificial body as the prophetic public presence. *Being* and *knowing* the body-self as "the light of the world" involves nothing less.

An episode from her life story exemplifies how Mrs. Hamer's body became a living sacrifice. On June 9, 1963, Mrs. Hamer and several other civil rights workers were enroute back to Sunflower County, Mississippi, after attending training sessions on voter registration in South Carolina. While briefly stopping over in Winona, Mississippi, the group was jailed for requesting service at the white lunch counter of the bus station. All but one teenaged girl was brutally beaten for their actions. Mrs. Hamer was especially tortured severely when the policeman discovered that she was "Fannie Lou Hamer from Ruleville—the same woman stirring up trouble in the Delta."[7] They proceeded to mentally abuse her, using expletives, and then brought two black inmates into the room to beat her. She asked them, "You mean you would do this to your own race?"[8] She was beaten by both black inmates, and later, when they became tired, two police officers continued the torture. By the end of the beating, Mrs. Hamer had blood clots and hard lumps from her head to her feet. In the months ahead she discovered her kidney had been permanently damaged.

Days later, when her trial began, Mrs. Hamer found the courage to speak truth to power. She told the jailer who had helped beat her a few days earlier and now was escorting her, "Do you people ever think or wonder how you'll feel when the time comes you'll have to meet God?"[9] She said the jailer's face showed signs of embarrassment and denial. Mrs. Hamer had the courage to render divine judgement to her assailant.

On another occasion, during an interview for *Sojourners Magazine*, Mrs. Hamer challenged the greater society when she said:

> *Christianity is being concerned about [others], not building a million-dollar church while people are starving right around the corner. Christ was a revolutionary person, out there where it was happening. That's what God is all about, and that's where I get my strength.*[10]

Once again, like a modern day prophet, Mrs. Hamer speaks the word of God in the public sphere exhorting us to work for the realization of God's love and justice.

Mrs. Hamer's life is an example of embodied ministry through her incarnate body-self and her sacrificial body-self. Her voice was the vehicle for her practice of a prophetic public presence. Using her voice she visited cotton fields by day and churches by night to

---

[4] Kay Mills, *This Little Light of Mine: The Life of Fannie Lou Hamer* (New York: Plume Book, 1993), p. 21.

[5] Ibid, p. 84.

[6] Ibid.

[7] Charles Marsh, *God's Long Summer: Stories of Faith and Civil Rights* (Princeton, New Jersey: Princeton University Press), p. 19.

[8] Ibid.

[9] Ibid, p. 23.

[10] Ibid, p. 33.

encourage workers and solicit voters with freedom songs and speeches.[11] Her voice was an indefatigable dominant presence in mass meetings around the state of Mississippi. During one such mass meeting at Tougaloo College, Mrs. Hamer took the pulpit by storm, giving testimony of her involvement in the movement. She later admonished her listeners on the true meaning of Christian discipleship saying,

> *People need to be serious about their faith in the Lord; it's all too easy to say, "Sure, 'I'm a Christian,' and talk a big game. But if you are not putting that claim to the test, where the rubber meets the road, then it's high time to stop talking about being a Christian. You can pray until you faint," she said, " but if you're not gonna get up and do something, God is not gonna put it in your lap."[12]*

Mrs. Hamer was abused in the Winona jail because she was a black woman with a voice.[13] She was hated for her voice with the same intensity as her colleagues and friends loved her voice and its power to rally them to action for the cause of justice. It was through Mrs. Hamer's voice that she inspired young civil rights workers in the Student Nonviolent Coordinating Committee to come to voice. These youth included fifteen-year-old June Johnson and seventeen-year-old Euvester Simpson, who were jailed with Mrs. Hamer in Winona. Both teens were young activists who organized and mobilized voter registration efforts during the 1964 Mississippi Freedom Summer Project.

In addition to Mrs. Hamer's voice and her ability to bring young activists to voice she demonstrated an unparalleled piety grounded in social justice. She possessed an untiring "belief in Jesus as friend and deliverer of the poor."[14] Her interpretation and application of scripture, the sacred music that she sung and the powerful prayers that she prayed are indicative of how her piety was tightly woven into the fabric of her prophetic persona.

The above snapshots of Mrs. Fannie Lou Hamer's life intend to demonstrate *good ministry* as embodied. Among the thematic practices that illustrate the *good ministry* that she embodied is the practice of prophetic public presence. Her body is the "light of the world," both its incarnation and sacrifice, guiding us to God's love and justice. She sings:

> *I've got the light of freedom*
> *I'm gonna let it shine.*
> *Jesus gave it to me,*
> *I'm gonna let it shine.*
> *Gonna shine all over the Delta,*
> *I'm gonna let it shine.*
> *Let it shine, let it shine, let it shine.[15]*

FOR REFLECTION

This paper defines *good ministry* as the incarnation of the human and divine Jesus who demonstrated the radical commitment of self-sacrifice in service of others. A lay person, Mrs. Fannie Lou Hamer, is lifted up as an exemplar of this form of *good ministry*. The practice of prophetic public presence, or her ability to challenge oppressors and motivate the oppressed to action, is central to her ministry.

1. What practices are essential for ordained clergy to empower laity for good ministry?

2. What does theological education need to consider in its preparation of clergy to demonstrate the practice of prophetic public presence? What's at stake if such preparation is not considered?

3. How might theological education prepare laity, its youth and adults, to practice prophetic public presence?

[11] Ibid, p. 25.

[12] Ibid.

[13] Ibid, p. 21.

[14] Ibid, p. 5.

[15] Ibid, p. 48.

7. TRIED AND TRUE, OLD AND NEW: PROCLAIMING THE WORD

Rebecca Chopp*

The question "What makes a good pastor?" deserves the right answer. Surely personal virtues, including compassion, courage, fortitude, and diligence, merit a place in the definition of what makes a minister "good." Depth formation in the faith, or a certain spiritual maturity, also contributes to being a good pastor. As a young minister, I once distributed a survey to see what my congregants wanted in a good minister: The unanimous answer was a strong spiritual life! Further, as in any profession, specific skills contribute to being a good clergyperson. Administration, preaching, counseling are all about being "good" in the ministry. And given the dramatic changes in the world, some special "new" answers might be provided: New skills in areas such as multi-faith dialogue and multimedia communication will be required to be a good pastor in the next decades. I confess that each one of these qualities is the right answer to the question: What makes a good minister?

As I stopped and started the writing of this brief essay due to my indecision about which right answer was the most important one, I realized that I kept coming back to an answer to the question born out of my tradition: What makes a minister good is knowing how to *proclaim the Word*. A minister may have great skills and virtues and may be on an incredible journey, but if she can't proclaim the Word, she just doesn't count as a good minister. I imagine this sounds harsh to modern and postmodern ears, but without being able to proclaim the Word, the ministers are left performing empty functions or, worse yet, to paraphrase Luther's most severe letter, in danger of becoming "Sneaks and Furtive Preachers."[1] Spirituality, dialogue, and vision receive substance through proclamation. When I look at what I know from Christian traditions, my twenty years in ministry

and theological education, and my experience participating in churches, the most important criterion for goodness is the ability to proclaim the Word of God. This is reinforced time and time again by church folks who ask me as a dean: Can you train your students to preach, please? (And church folks know the difference between preaching and public speaking.)

For Luther, the Word founds, creates, and sustains the community. Despite our democratic assumptions that community is formed by a critical mass of caring, committed individuals, this is not at all Luther's view. The Word initiates and funds Christian community. And the community's real role and obligation is to proclaim the Word. All other ministries and services flow from and through the community's proclaiming God's glory in the world, or, to say it in Wesleyan language, testifying of God's love in and of the world. Schleiermacher and Barth, to take two great moderns who disagreed on many things, agreed completely that the Word creates the church. Barth's version of this basic truth: "The community is created and confronted by the Word of God. It is *communio sanctorum*, the communion of saints, because it is *congregatio fidelium*, the gathering of the faithful. As such it is the *coniuratio testium*, the confederation of witnesses who may and must speak because they believe."[2] The *proclamation* of the Word is important because faith must be continuously nourished in the context of a Word-drenched community. Faith is not a once-for-all implant, but an ongoing relationship that depends upon proclamation for its subsistence, growth, and expression. To quote Luther, "Since the church owes to the Word its birth, nourishment, protection, and strength, it is obvious that it cannot be without the Word; if it is without the Word it ceases to be the church."[3]

The proclamation of the Word, the obligation of the church, is not simply expressed in preaching but also in the sacraments, sacrifice, intercession, the binding and

---

* Rebecca Chopp is President of Colgate University, Hamilton, N.Y. At the time she wrote this essay, she was Dean of Yale Divinity School and Titus Street Professor of Theology and Culture.

[1] Quoted in Brian A. Gerrish, "Priesthood and Ministry: Luther's Fifth Means of Grace," in *The Old Protestantism and the New: Essays on Reformation Heritage* (Chicago: University of Chicago Press, 1982), p. 92. I am indebted to this article for my understanding of Luther's use of functional and institutional arguments for ministry.

[2] Karl Barth, *Evangelical Theology: An Introduction*, trans. Grover Foley (Grand Rapids, Mich.: Eerdmans, 1963), p. 38.

[3] Quoted in Gerrish, *The Old Protestantism and the New*, p. 95.

loosing of sins, and the judging of doctrine. For Luther, the minister, authorized by function as well as by divine institution, is responsible for public proclamation. Needless to say, what makes for a good minister is the ability and wisdom to proclaim the Word! Naturally, the good news will take various forms and will be expressed in different ways at different times. Still, the minister's obligation, like that of her congregation, is the ability to fully proclaim the Word in the world.

Why do I insist so strongly on this dated language? First of all, by grounding ministry and the church in the proclamation of the Word, we end up making ministry a theological profession. Proclamation means that in everything the minister does she has to reflect theologically, tracing and amplifying God's spirit and interpreting it in sign and action and speech. Good ministers are those who know the Word and know how to feel it and express it. Secondly, proclamation of the Word, by which Protestantism means the Good News of God for us in this place and time, is needed by the world. In the weeks following September 11, various churches and schools expressed the importance of Christian public speech and recognized the opportunity for the church to offer a moral voice in the public. But, as one friend said to me on September 15, "What shall I say now that folks will listen?" I think if we are honest, most of us are not sure of the moral discourse the church will offer. Does the contemporary church know the good news to proclaim it? Thirdly, proclamation has been reduced to preaching as some kind of interesting (and hopefully) brief speech every Sunday morning. Preaching is one expression of proclamation and needs to be woven into the Word in all its forms and images. But when preaching substitutes for a deeper, broader life as proclamation of the Word, anorexic Christianity exists. Fourthly, without being good at proclaiming the Word, the pastor may reduce his congregation to simply an association of religiously interested individuals and not, as Luther insisted, feed the faith of the church continually on the Word. Ministers who don't proclaim the Word end up with interesting religious affiliations but not churches.

What does all this mean for our day-to-day work in ministry and in theological education? Is this just the crabbiness of a middle-aged professor who engages in

Ministers who don't proclaim the Word end up with interesting religious affiliations but not churches.

sentimental tributes to theologians no longer read by anyone? It is probably easier to complain about the lack of proclamation of the Word than to point to the ways we know how proclamation of the Word occurs as a sign of good ministry. But I think there are at least three ways to identify an appropriate contemporary understanding of how ministers proclaim the Word of God.

First of all, if the Word feeds faith, then the good minister nurtures and cultivates Christian community. For Luther, Barth, and Schleiermacher, the church was in some sense "prior" to the individual. The Word shapes persons through ecclesial practices: Eucharist, baptism, prayers, and hospitality, all of which build the community and form the individual Christian. But the minister is not simply a Christian trainer of practices for muscular community and marathoners of the faith; the good minister ensures that the practices building community are interpreted, judged, and extended through the Word. One of the reasons I prefer Luther's unique blend of justification for ordained ministry through both an argument of divine institution and an argument of functionality is that only by holding these together do we have a minister whose sacred role is to privilege the community as the vehicle of the Word. To say it even more traditionally, we need pastors who understand the community (and not the minister) as the primary vehicle of God in the world, and we need ministers who build this community in and through the Word.

Second, within the church the minister needs to ensure that the congregation orders its life together in the Spirit. The minister in this role finds ultimate in penultimate and judges the penultimate in the midst of the ultimate. Augustine spoke of ordering our loves and desires in God and loving things not in themselves but in God. The minister helps her community and individuals in her community do that. Valuing and ordering as basic spiritual principles depend, I believe, upon an aesthetic sense of the holy. This may mean pointing to a sense of the whole, or a feeling of absolute dependence, or being in awe of gracious mystery, but the ministry needs to make sure the congregation lives in relation to Love. Ordering and valuing as a Christian way of life mean interpreting past traditions and learning how they valued and ordered lives in relation to the holy. I think many mainline congregations fail at this and many ministers make way too few demands in this area. Johann Baptist Metz is, sadly, only being descriptive when he observes that the problem with the church is not that

Third, a spiritual leader develops a narrative imagination of God's love in and for the world. A gospel founded in resurrection-crucifixion-incarnation is one that sees new ways of being and doing in all things. We need spiritual leaders who can help persons find compelling visions in which to live and who can proclaim words of hope and freedom that are not the ways of the world. Martha Nussbaum talks about the need for the "narrative imagination," by which she means imaginations so formed that other ways of being can be seen.[6] And we need new versions of Christian narrative imagination. The Beatitudes, whatever else they are, are a statement about how the Christian sees the world as it should be and in this sight lives his or her life. Karl Rahner wrote of the priest as poet, and how desperately we need ministers who live out of a poetic imagination and aid their congregations in forming poetic imagination. The task of the pastor is not only to shape imagination for the community, but also to help the community produce new visions for the common good and for the world. The old WASP vision of the common good will not work any longer, but surely Scripture, tradition, and contemporary experience are filled with resources for a new Christian vision of the common good, not just a vision of the Christian common good. The prophetic role arises out of the Christian moral imagination and not, as is so commonly practiced, vice versa. Proclaiming the Word is part and parcel of the Christian imagination that fuels our service and witness.

It is old and new, tried and true. In the beginning, in the end, and for all the time in between: What makes a minister a good minister is his or her ability to proclaim God's Word.

FOR REFLECTION

1. How do you understand the nature of "proclaiming the good news" in the contemporary period?

2. What is your vision of community and how is the community founded on good news?

3. Describe how imagination functions in preaching and the role of the imagination in your church?

we have demanded too much but that we have required too little.[4] Theology is a process of ordering (as well as building and envisioning) values through the interpretation of doctrines and beliefs. Doctrines, fundamentally, are the capacities we have for experiencing and seeing the world in a Christian way. As such, doctrines are shaped through practices and life together in the church. But doctrines must be taught, analyzed, reinterpreted, and wrestled with just as any act of love is a continuing process to find the right language to interpret it and guide it. Good doctrines order values and, as Kathryn Tanner has rightly suggested, are constantly being renegotiated.[5]

---

[4]   Johann Baptist Metz, *The Emergent Church*, trans. Peter Mann (New York: Crossroad, 1981).

[5]   Kathryn Tanner, *Theories of Culture: A New Agenda for Theology* (Minneapolis: Fortress Press, 1997), pp. 144-155.

[6]   Martha C. Nussbaum, "The Narrative Imagination," *Cultivating Humanity: A Classical Defense of Reform in Liberal Education* (Cambridge: Harvard University Press, 1997), pp. 85-112.

8. Principle, Priority, and Practice

Brad Ronnell Braxton*

I. The Principle: "Good ministry entails a commitment to personal holiness."

Unless we are careful, ministers can turn holiness into a "professional duty" rather than a personal discipline. As a "watchperson" stationed upon the tower, the minister constantly "looks outward." Effective ministry also demands that the watchperson turn the gaze inward. The good minister must frequently interrogate herself, perhaps uttering the words of that African American hymn, "Search me, Lord. Shine the light from heaven on my soul."

In *The Scarlet Thread*, Gardner Taylor uses the Mississippi River to illustrate the importance of the inward gaze for ministry. The Mississippi River starts out enormously small, even inconspicuously, in the North. When it reaches the Mississippi Delta, however, it is nearly a mile wide. Taylor uses the metaphor to suggest that public power in ministry has its genesis in inconspicuous places—in the private, disciplined attempts of the preacher to live a consecrated life. Often, it is not the so-called "scarlet sins" that, in the language of Hebrews, "doth so easily beset" the preacher, but the more subtle sins.

For example, a subtle sin against which ministers must guard is intellectual laziness. Our commitment to love God with our minds must not *terminate* on *commencement* day from divinity school. Another sin that can undermine a preacher's sense of consecration is "savior behavior and pastor worship." In ecclesial traditions where strong, minister-centered leadership is the norm, there is often a fine line between honoring the minister and making the minister an object of sacred veneration.

With perspicacity, Charles Spurgeon wrote, "It will be in vain for me to stock my library or organize societies or project schemes, if I neglect the culture of myself; for books and agencies, and systems are only remotely the instruments of my holy calling; my own spirit, soul, and body are my nearest machinery for sacred service."[1] Good ministry humbly leads people into "asymptotic holiness." An asymptote is a straight line always approaching but never meeting a curve. So it is with the minister's quest for holiness. Our inability to perfectly embody holiness does not absolve us from the responsibility of perpetually approaching it.

II. The Priority: "Good ministry knows that not every urgent matter is important but every important matter is urgent."

Since ministers perform sundry tasks, the establishment of priorities is crucial for effective ministry. In 1 Corinthians 15, Paul clearly articulated his ministerial priorities. He declares, "I handed on to you as of *first importance* what I in turn had received, that Christ died for our sins in accordance with the scriptures, and that he was buried, and that he was raised on the third day in accordance with the scriptures."

The Greek phrase in 1 Corinthians 15:3 that is translated "as of first importance" (en prōtois) can also be rendered temporally. One might translate it: "I handed on to you *in the first instance*." Thus, Paul may be saying that proclaiming the gospel was the first thing he did upon his arrival in Corinth, or he may be saying that proclaiming the gospel was of utmost importance. I think that Paul intended both nuances. Preaching for Paul was primary in two ways. It was both the first thing he did and from his perspective the most important thing he did. In his apostleship, Paul set priorities, and the execution of those priorities claimed his best energies.

Good ministers can infer an important spiritual axiom from Paul's words. The most important things should claim our attention and energy first. Unfortunately, so often in ministry, the things that we get to first are not the things that are most important. To use the words of another, most ministers need to be freed from the "tyranny of the urgent." Not everything in ministry that is urgent is important, but on the contrary the important things should be urgent.

Too many ministers have anemic devotional lives, chaotic family lives, and barren preaching ministries because of an inability to set and maintain priorities. Many ministers declare that they want their congregations to grow spiritually, but then these ministers do not zealously

---

* Brad R. Braxton is the Jessie Ball duPont Assistant Professor of Homiletics and Biblical Studies, Wake Forest University Divinity School, Winston-Salem, N.C.

[1] Charles H. Spurgeon, *Lectures to my Students* (Grand Rapids: Zondervan Publishing House, 1958) 7-8.

guard their own moments of solitude with God. Other ministers declare that they want a church where "the family" is a priority, but these same ministers place *every* church crisis, real or imagined, above the needs of their own families. Still other ministers set effective preaching as a priority. They, however, then agree to serve on every community board and to accept every invitation to civic gatherings, leaving them precious little time for prayer, critical study of the scripture, and careful attention to their homiletical language.

In short, one cannot say "yes" to one's ministry priorities unless one is also able to say "no" to other (sometimes worthwhile) obligations.

III. Practice: "By equipping the saints, good ministry creates good ministry."

Effective ministerial leaders know that "good ministry" is ultimately the responsibility of the *entire church*. The myriad tasks of ministry always exceed the minister's personal giftedness and training. Thus, God providentially has deposited gifts for ministry in every person who makes up a local congregation. Good ministry assists congregants in identifying and employing their gifts of ministry for the welfare of the church and community. In the language of Ephesians, good ministry equips the saints.

To equip is to emancipate. The minister is liberated *from* the dreadful feeling that she has to do everything. The congregation is liberated *for* disciplined action. By equipping the saints, the breadth and depth of a congregation's influence can grow exponentially. I offer a specific example from my ministry.

During my pastorate at Douglas Memorial Community Church in Baltimore, I began a Wednesday Bible study that met at noon and 6 p.m. The attendance between the two Wednesday sessions would range from a hundred to nearly two hundred—in a congregation where three hundred to four hundred worshipped on Sunday. To have 25 percent of the worshipping congregation in serious study on Wednesday afforded me a golden opportunity to equip the saints.

During a yearlong study of Luke's Gospel, I devoted two months in that curriculum to teaching students about the rigors and rewards of a preaching ministry. Though I was the "hired hand" for preaching, I contended that every Christian should have at least one sermon, and I set out to teach my students how to create and preach it.

For several weeks, I taught a mini-homiletics course, discussing the various elements of persuasive Christian preaching. Then, I assigned each person the task of writing a brief sermon from Luke 9. For six weeks, the members of the Bible study preached their sermons in class. The depth of these sermons blessed all the participants in the Bible study.

I selected the best four sermons preached by women and the best four preached by men, and later that year, during our celebrations of Women's Day and Men's Day, those lay persons preached their sermons in spirit-filled services of worship. Not only did this exercise increase parishioners' understanding of (and even empathy for) the demands of preaching, but also from this experience, one man in our congregation received his call to professional ministry. He is now pursuing his theological studies in seminary. Ministry had created ministry and even another minister.

FOR REFLECTION

1. Define "holiness." Then, identify the personal and corporate practices that either encourage or impede one's commitment to holiness. Explore why the practices are beneficial or detrimental to one's sense of holiness.

2. A prominent minister once suggested that two of the most important "rooms" for any minister are the "study" and the "prayer closet." In the "study," the minister connects with God through deep reflection. In the "prayer closet," the minister connects with God through heart-felt petition. What are the dangers of a minister visiting only one of these rooms to the exclusion of the other? What are the benefits of the minister spending ample time in both "rooms"?

3. There is an old maxim that states, "Lips will say anything, but behavior never lies." Often clergy state their ministry priorities but then undermine these priorities with their practices. Reflect on a minister and congregation that you know well. What do the *practices* of this minister indicate about her/his ministry priorities? Are the stated priorities and the actual practices congruent? What can this congruence or incongruity say about one's idea of God and of the church?

4. "Ministry" is not the responsibility of any one person but is, in fact, the vocation of the whole church. Identify creative ways that clergy might better equip the laity to carry out church ministries such as preaching/teaching, evangelism, visitation, spiritual direction, local and international poverty relief, community support (e.g., child care and elder care, HIV/AIDS support groups). In your estimation, are there any practices of ministry in which the laity should not be involved? If so, what are they, and explore why you feel this way.

9. Pastor, Lay Ministers and Community Amid the Changes of History

Thomas F. O'Meara, O.P.*

How can we educate and support pastorally successful ministers? My comments on this theme come from the point of view of a teacher and a theologian and not from a more proper source, a pastor. Since I do not labor in the parish, I asked a pastor of a very large Mexican-American parish in Chicago about being one. He answered: "A good pastor provides a vision, a vision theological and communal as well as administrative. The pastor is the source of unity for the many people and the various ministers in the parish; he unites different points of view even as he leads all to a deeper view of the church, one faithful to the Gospel, one engaged with society. The pastor promotes others as ministers in different areas; that promotion involves attracting, identifying, educating and preparing, and supporting others in the ministry, whether that be a half dozen full-time ministers or six hundred parishioners."

How would some theological perspectives of interest to me support this voice of experience?

(1) Pastoral ministry begins with the healthy and evangelical conviction that ministry serves people and the reign of God; like its teaching Lord, the church too is a servant and does not control or monopolize God's presence.

To serve people as a citizen of the kingdom implies a respect for both realities: the individual, and the Spirit's presence. Serving someone begins with seeking to understand what men and women are saying about their lives, and then glimpsing how grace might be contacting them. And too one must understand something of the times so that the minister may ponder what the Holy Spirit is doing in this age, in this church at this time.

We live in a time of fundamentalisms, of the religious ideologies and cultic behavior that so irritated Jesus in their arrogant isolation and display. A fundamentalism seeks to constrict and control the kingdom of God. Each fundamentalism is ultimately a psychological as well as a theological stance: thus the psychological drive-system of fundamentalisms lies deeper than being a Muslim or an orthodox Jew or a Baptist or a Roman Catholic. Forms and things and creeds and rites are necessary for human religion, but fundamentalism rigidly focuses on a few externals of the recent past, turning grace to magic and involving discipleship in the condemnation of others. The fundamentalist is by nature a sectarian, and the sect exists to turn individuals into theatrical stars of religion. Preaching and liturgy, however, should aid people to accept the liberating orientation of Jesus' teaching and the Spirit's Word, to see how what is concrete and verbal and sacramental is transparent to God's grace, to engage the senses without being magical. The openness and mystery of God's kingdom served by the church invites broad worlds of searching men and women.

One learns about the kingdom of God from Jesus' preaching and learns about people approaching the kingdom from the narratives of the Gospels. Insight for serving graced people comes from the theories of great theologians and spiritual writers, although theology also comes from presentations in fiction and other arts or from biographies. They tell us about how God works in people. The individual person in the reign of God is ultimate. While the church expresses and makes grace concrete, God also moves sovereignly and silently, mysterious and ceaselessly through the psyches of all people. As Thomas Aquinas observed, "God has not tied grace to the sacraments." Some theology of understanding the mystery of the reign of God centered in the historical Jesus but present in the world also to those apart from churches is central to ministry today.

(2) The pastor is no longer a solitary minister or priest but the teaching and liturgical coordinator of a ministering parish.

For the past thirty-five years, the Catholic Church has been in the midst of the expansion and diversification of ministry in the parish and the diocese. Very rapidly, in the years after Vatican II ministry

---

* Thomas O'Meara teaches in the Department of Theology of the University of Notre Dame.

changed, changed by expanding into ministries of education, liturgy, and social justice; by professionalization in campus ministry and health care ministry; by the development of diocesan offices directing ministry. It was not bishops or theologians or charismatic figures who altered the format of the Catholic parish but the ideas of Vatican II about baptism, ministries for all Christians, and parish life, a variety of liturgical, educational, and social enterprises in parish. There was suddenly lots to do and large numbers of people interested in ministry, liturgy, and education. The very model of ministry changed, changed in its patterns—theological, ecclesiological and professional—of what was done and who did it. The parish of 1962 was little different from a parish in 962. The concrete form of the parish of 1962 or of 962, however, does not, by and large, resemble the Catholic parish today in most of the United States in its post-conciliar style.

The pastor directs and attracts others into the ministry of the parish and enables them through his or her own considerable ministry. The passages by St. Paul listing different kinds of ministries and relating the Spirit's charisms to people at work for the church speak directly to a parish today. The new model involves a staff of full-time ministers, a community of serving ministers, led by the pastor, with their own education, expertise, natural gifts, and commission or rites.[1]

The Body of Christ has many gifts and services, and they are not in competition. The pastoral support of lay ecclesial ministry should take seriously the incorporation of lay ecclesial ministers into the diocese in terms of adequate salary, benefits, appreciation, along with support and guidance in the spiritual life. Those serving in various ministries are not replacements for a lack of priests, and ministry should never be a "job." Not just the ordained but all those serving the presence of the Spirit are bound by a spiritual life, for ministry and spirituality go joined together. There must be Christian life-styles for all in the ministry, ways of living the Gospel that are neither monastic nor secular.

(3) Dynamic moments, partly from the past, but rediscovered and energizing the present, are influencing the church today.

Four trajectories, four dynamic movements from Christian periods, push the expansion of ministry: (i) a re-appropriation of the Pauline theology of the Body of Christ with varied ministries for the local church in a pattern of concentric circles of ministry around the pastor and sustained by the Spirit; (ii) the inability of the single distinction, social and ecclesiastical, between clergy and laity to sum up today's church; (iii) the ministry of women; (iv) the passage beyond the recent past of private devotions and spirituality to a liturgical, educated, and socially engaged church. One of these dynamics would bring problems enough. This convergence of epochal changes explains why in the past decade or so not a few ecclesiastical leaders have chosen to pretend that none of these new directions exist and to retire, condemning "modernity," into a world of the sacristy storeroom. It can be a help and consolation to understand the extent of these changes, a rare historical alteration of the church in history. The Spirit has a plan—apparently it is the reintroduction of broad ministerial activity in the local church—and history never goes backwards.

Finding the format of parish ministry is a work-in-progress. The reality of size and numbers is central. The population of American Catholics is rising beyond sixty-five million toward seventy-four million; through baptism and confirmation a hundred thousand adults enter the American church each year, potential recipients of education and of a call to ministry. The number of Catholics is large and people want to become involved in the ministry, and yet the number of diocesan priests continues to decline. One must face the approaching year 2005 as the edge of crisis. Then there will be very few religious women in active ministry (a reduction from many tens of thousands), and the bulk of American priests will be between sixty-five and seventy-five years old. There is a lack of planning for what the American church will be in ten years. A new pontificate will face a series of pressing issues among which will be married priests and women deacons. At the same time, there has been and is great interest among young Catholics in ministry—but in ecclesial lay ministry, and often in temporary ministry. As some have pointed out, there has never in the Christian church been such an abundance of ministers as today—and yet from some perspectives there are few.

---

[1] See Winfried Haunerland, "The Heirs of the Clergy? The New Pastoral Ministries and the Reform of the Minor Orders," *Worship* 75 (2001) 305-320.

A second, practical issue is the new situation in ministerial education. A dozen or so universities, colleges or theological schools have lost their monopoly over advanced education in ministry through full-time or summer programs, and local programs have multiplied. Thus the American Catholic Church finds itself with various programs of education for ministry: local programs, programs in theological schools, and programs in colleges and universities; programs gaining certificates or programs gaining graduate degrees. The coordination of these programs and their mutual service is yet to be pursued.

The pastor serves in the midst of these changes, sometimes faced with unreal demands by both society and by church administration. Strange that while a clericalism returns for a few and bureaucracies seek to curtail the local church, parish life continues in the conciliar directions where people and the Spirit and history conspire to fashion Christian community.

FOR REFLECTION

1. Are lay ministers who are prepared theologically and pastorally for important ministry well integrated into the parish and local church; does that integration include not only just financial compensation but an inclusion in the theological and spiritual development of the ordained?

2. Does the "professionalization" of lay ministers imply something secular, or is that professionalization the recognition that ministry should be the responsibility of men and women who are well prepared, in various ways?

3. Are churches aware of the recent expansion of ministerial education, of new programs and new goals for part-time and full-time ministries?

4. What are the limits of educating ministers for a particular church in an ecumenical or intra-denominational context.

10. COLLEGIAL, COLLABORATIVE, AND SHARED

Zeni Fox*

What constitutes good ministry? This is, indeed, a complex question; so many aspects of ministry could be considered. We could approach this theologically, viewing ministry as a continuation of the work Jesus began and considering the variety of ministries which flow from his diverse roles, such as Teacher, or Healer. Or, we could take the individual minister as our starting point, and weigh the importance of faith and attentiveness to the presence of God, of human and social development and pastoral skills, perhaps even of the level of energy for the task, predicated on good self-care. The community, too, could be the focus of attention. The larger community of the denomination could be studied, the vision it offers for the furthering of the Kingdom of God and the support it provides for ministers and local communities. Or, the local community, parish or congregation, could be considered, its spiritual well-being, the history of its commitment to the Gospel, its ministerial involvement by many, its relationship with the ministers—supportive, participatory.

We were invited to focus on one or several points that are important to the discussion. The choice of my approach flows from my background and experience. I am a theologian whose particular area of study has been lay ministry. For fifteen years I have served as a teacher and director of lay ministry at a Roman Catholic seminary. My judgments about good ministry are based in part on the stories of many of our graduates, on research about vibrant parishes and congregations and on study of the tradition of the Church. My personal experience as a life-long Church member, and earlier in my life as a Church worker in several settings, also shapes my perspective.

Good ministry by an individual, ordained or lay, is rooted in community. Communities nurture the faith of the young, provide the context in which a call to ministry is discerned, and validate that call. Communities provide the structures for preparation for ministry, such as seminaries, field-education sites, and mentors. Communities nourish the identity of the minister, providing an important part of the validation needed in order to sustain the sense of self *as* minister. And communities are the context of ministry. However much an individual may think of ministry as "mine," no matter how one-on-one a dimension of ministry he/she may perform, it is as a member of a faith tradition that one is a public person in the Church, a minister. Theologically, we recognize that God called forth a community—Israel, the People of God, and the Church, the People of God. In the desert, each Israelite did not receive a personal map to the Promised Land; they traveled together. Or, were lost in the desert. The followers of Jesus, rooted in this tradition, understand themselves as a Koinonia. Good ministry is rooted in the life of the People of God, in faithful relationship with the denomination, with fellow ministers and with the parish or congregation or other entity with and within which one ministers.

Good ministry is collegial, collaborative, shared. (The definition offered by Sofield and Juliano is helpful: "collaboration… is the identification, release and union of the gifts of all baptized persons." It applies to the work of a leader with the people, and to the work of various leaders, together.[1]) The models are there in the New Testament, to inspire and challenge. In Acts, we read of the Twelve, and the Seven, the relationship of the individuals to the whole affirmed more definitively than the individuals themselves. We also read that the Twelve consulted with the community and called on all to assist in the process of identifying additional leaders for ministry. Paul, in his letters, records over a hundred people by name who were associated with him in his work. And when he refers to them collectively he says "my fellow workers" or "my brothers" (this despite the fact that many were women). Paul, so insistent on his call by the Lord, so anxious to state that he, too, was an apostle, gives us a picture of a ministry performed together with, and in ongoing relationship to, other ministers.

In our present cultural context emphasis on collaborative ministry takes on new importance. One reason is that as societies throughout the world have become more participatory and as people in the United States have matured in a democratic life-style, institutions have changed their ways of exercising leadership. "Command and control" functions are still important but now a

---

* Zeni Fox is Associate Professor of Pastoral Theology, Immaculate Conception Seminary, Seton Hall University, South Orange, N.J.

[1] Longhlan Sofield and Carroll Juliano, *Collaborative Ministry, Skills and Guidelines* (Notre Dame, Ind.: Ave Maria Press, 1987), p. 11.

more participatory style is favored and team work is emphasized. A second reason is that as ever-increasing specialization makes people more dependent on the expertise of others, a consistent style of collaborative working and shared decision making is necessary for effective functioning. The social trends create expectations in people in the society, both ministers and those they serve for collaborative ministry, and the specialized gifts of staffs and members of congregations require effective working together, if they are to be maximized.

All ministry has as one of its goals forming community, inviting people into relationship with one another and, both collectively and individually, with God. All ministry has as a goal building up the Body of Christ, nurturing the community of the saints. All ministry has as a goal assisting the community in its task of continuing the work Jesus began, as the community he called into being, disciples, together. Collaborative ministry models this communal life in its style of working together, the leadership one with the other, the leadership with the community. Collaborative ministry values the relationship of all, one to the other; it is not focused only on task, on doing, but also on being, on the shared life of the community.

The second half of our question is, what creates the conditions for good ministry? What creates the conditions for collaborative ministry? There are two parts to the answer to this question: first, what helps collaborative ministry in itself, and second, what helps to form leaders who will be collaborative?

Collaborative ministry is possible in denominations and parishes or congregations who value it, both theoretically and practically. Theoretically, the word "collaboration" may not appear in any official teachings, but the conviction that the task of continuing the work of Jesus belongs to all the people must be clearly enunciated. Official and informal teaching cannot so emphasize the role of a few as to effectively minimize the role of the larger body. Practically, attention to the building of structures, and education in the skills needed for collaboration, is needed. In some religious communities, such as the Quakers, there is a long tradition of collegiality, and of mechanisms for assisting the development of consensus in a group. (For example, if someone cannot agree with the perspective of the group, after a point he/she steps aside to allow the consensus to go forward.) Some communities have traditions which have limited collegial functioning. In these communities even if the vision changes the learned behaviors will be slower to change, and much attention to the development of structures and skills will be needed.

Collaborative ministry requires ministerial leadership prepared to work collaboratively. Again, it is the life of the community itself which nurtures and prepares its ministers; collaborative judicatories, parishes/congregations and seminaries model, and encourage, the vision and skills needed for collaborative ministry. Such institutions demonstrate a valuing of the gifts of members of the community, an engagement of diverse persons in a variety of roles, developed structures for collaborative functioning and theological reflection on the lived life of the community. In seminary education and in a denomination's educational programs attention must be given to teaching the skills needed for collaborative leadership, for drawing many into active participation in the ministry of the Church. Such programs should assist participants to examine cultural, ecclesial, and personal tendencies that hinder collaboration. For example, the competitive norms and structures of male dominance in the culture need to be examined, as should the ecclesial pattern of yielding to the desire of individuals and groups to be dependent. Because effective collaboration depends on realistic perceptions of and a healthy attitude toward power, personal exploration of this aspect of life is necessary. And, because collaboration also depends on mutual trust, self-knowledge about the ability to grant and receive trust is important. Education about collaboration should also explore the difficulties inherent in such a style, including the unwillingness to name negativities and the danger of not providing leadership. (The task of the leader to self-define, to provide a vision, to take risks, should not be co-opted by collegiality.)

Given our tradition, and the signs of the times, one dimension of good ministry is that it be collaborative. Collaborative ministry itself creates the primary condition for collaborative ministry. In addition, intentional activities are needed to further understanding of, and skills for, collaborative ministry.

FOR REFLECTION

1. Think of an example of good collaborative ministry you have experienced, as a member of the leadership team or the community with which it ministered. What was "good"? Why did the collaboration work?

2. In a community you know well, what structures assist collaboration? How skilled in collaboration are the members of the community? On a scale of 1-10, with 10 high, how would you rate the community as a setting to learn about collaborative ministry? Why?

3. What do you personally see as the strengths of collaborative ministry? The limitations?

11. At the Foot of the Cross

Kathleen A. Cahalan*

When we see good ministry in action we generally recognize it in powerful preaching, uplifting liturgy, competent teaching, caring pastoral touch, and passionate service. But what do all these practices of ministry hold in common that can claim them as "good"? What characteristics are present each time good ministry is practiced? What is the biblical and theological foundation that forms the basis for good ministry? Are there important benchmarks that might help us to describe, understand, and evaluate good ministry? At the end of the day, how can we as ministers and ministering communities know we have accomplished this thing called "good ministry"?

Like the roots of a tree, the rich soil that forms a river delta, or the foundation stones of a house, good ministry has an inner core, a foundation that makes it vital, abundant, and strong. In the Roman Catholic community we have a tradition of social teachings that focuses on the theological and moral analysis of the social, political, and economic order. This core set of ideas arises from the Church's mission to the world—a mission that begins in the worshipping community of faith but extends and reaches beyond its boundaries. The great social encyclical of the Second Vatican Council, *Gaudium et Spes*, expresses the Church's solidarity with the whole human family in this way: "The joy and hope, the grief and anguish of the men of our time, especially of those who are poor or afflicted in any way, are the joy and hope, the grief and anguish of the followers of Christ as well." The Church's ministry, then, is not faithful to its mission if it is believes that ministry is focused on its own internal matters; rather, the measure of good ministry is the extent to which the community's worship, preaching, teaching, and pastoral care creates faithful disciples for service in the world. How, then, might the biblical and theological values that form the basis for the Catholic social teachings help us to define good ministry?

Human persons are created in the image of God: Good ministry begins in the recognition that every human person is created in the image of God (Gen 1:26), an image that is manifest in the whole person—the body, social relations, and historical existence as well as our capacities for knowledge, freedom, and conscience. Regardless of any human act, good ministry recognizes that the *imago Dei* is the source and ground for each person's capacity to respond to God in faith, and to their neighbor in loving service. In recognizing God's image in all humanity, good ministry knows no limits: it fosters dignity and respect for life from conception to death.

In reality, however, we fail to recognize each person's dignity, and we fail to respect life as a gift from God. In that sense, good ministry knows sin—our capacity to reject God and the life intended by God. Good ministry recognizes the endless ways that sin corrupts and controls our thoughts and actions and reaches pervasively into our hearts and communities. But good ministry does not fear to name sin: it proclaims the brokenness, destruction, and misery that we heap upon ourselves through our own lack of respect for the self, the neighbor, and for God.

Good ministry, then, is always reconciling. It can never abandon the sinner, nor leave any to believe that sin is the final word about humanity. Seeking to reconcile the sinner to both God and the community, good ministry invites people into a freedom born of God's love, a love made present through the indwelling of God's image. The principle of human dignity means, as Helen Prejan has stated, that "[e]very human being is more than the worse thing they have ever done." Good ministry, itself, begins in the waters of Baptism, initiating each of us into a life of ongoing conversion away from sin into the fullness of life in Jesus Christ—the *imago Dei* transformed into the *imiatio Christi* (Gal 4:9).

We are social creatures, made for relationship with one another: Human persons are fundamentally social beings, created for community with one another and for communion with the Triune God. Good ministry

---

* Kathleen Cahalan is Assistant Professor, Pastoral Theology and Ministry, St. John's University School of Theology and Seminary, Collegeville, Minn.

fosters the Church as the People of God, those who know themselves as bound in covenant relationship with God and neighbor. Insofar as the People of God are baptized into the Mystical Body of Christ, Christians become "a sacrament—a sign and instrument, that is, of communion with God and unity among all men." (*Lumen Gentium*).

Good ministry encourages full and active participation by the community in the Church's witness and service in the world. Good ministry arises from fellowship among Christ's disciples who gather around the table of the Lord's Supper celebrating the "mysteries of our faith." By sharing in the Eucharist, Christians are members of a ministerial community of discipleship, service and witness, and by this fellowship, become bread and wine for the world.

> *It seems good ministry cannot play favorites or choose who to serve, for in our midst is both the criminal and the victim.*

Solidarity with the poor and the vulnerable: Good ministry serves the needs of the poor because Christ served the poor, and through that service, the Church serves Christ (Mt 25:30). Because God favors the lowly and the poor, good ministry practices a "preferential option for the poor." The Latin American bishops define three ways in which the Church serves the poor: by denouncing material poverty—"a lack of the goods of this world necessary to live worthily"—as sin; through preaching and living spiritual poverty as humble and self-giving love; and by committing to a life of voluntary material poverty (*Medell'n Documents*, 1968). Good ministry is both pastoral and prophetic. It seeks to remedy hunger, homelessness, and abuse through direct service to those in need as well as change in the social and economic conditions that destroy life and dishonor God.

Good ministry brings consolation and hope to the physically and spiritually vulnerable as well. By serving the weak, caring for the sick, and accompanying the dying, good ministry stands amidst all human vulnerability. It does so from an interesting vantage point— from the perspective of those standing at the foot of the cross. Good ministry is ready to walk with all who are innocent victims of disease, tragedy, and the world's injustice. And in the depths of humanity's misery, good ministry proclaims an amazing message about God's healing salvation that overcomes all suffering and death through Christ's cross and resurrection.

But just as good ministry stands with innocent human suffering, it also recognizes the two criminals executed with Jesus (Luke 23:32-43). It seems good ministry

cannot play favorites or choose who to serve, for in our midst is both the criminal and the victim. Good ministry does not abandon the sinner, the guilty one, the criminal. As Christ welcomed the dying criminal next to him on the cross into the Kingdom, good ministry walks with the guilty—even at times the enemy—offering them the good news of forgiveness and salvation (Mt 5:43-44).

Solidarity is cousin to stewardship: Good ministry is solidarity with both the human family and all of God's creation. The idea of solidarity expresses the interdependence of all earthly life—a reality that is increasingly endangered by the tremendous cost we exact on the earth's resources. Beyond our own households and communities of faith, the Eucharist calls Christians into solidarity with creation that means a life of ongoing sacrifice—our total self-giving to God—for the sake of God's world.

Because human life is dependent upon the whole of creation, solidarity expresses itself through stewardship, the wise and grateful use of God's gifts. One of the most important gifts we receive from God is our vocation, a particular calling to share our gifts and charisms in the community. Good ministry is vocation-centered. It attends to each person's vocation—inviting, encouraging, and calling forth the gifts to be shared. A community that practices the stewardship of vocations, will be prudent stewards of all God's gifts.

Good ministry is always local—and for the sake of the world: The central tasks of ministry—handing on the faith, proclaiming the gospel, caring for souls, and worshipping God—begin in what the tradition calls the "domestic church," the family. The family is the first school of prayer and virtue and, likewise, the first and primary context of Christian ministry and service. The local church, present in the parish and neighborhood, realizes the fullness of the Church's mission and ministry. Using the Catholic principle of subsidiarity, the congregation must not "do" for the family what it can (and should) do for itself, and the diocese (judicatory or denomination) must not "do" for the congregation what it can do itself. Those structures and organizations beyond the local community can serve it best by nurturing the fullest manifestation of the Church's mission and ministry in that place.

Good ministry can never attend only to the good of one's own family or faith community, however. We are continually called beyond our local relationships and interests to the concerns of our society and world. Good ministry embraces fundamental social values in support of the common good, "in order that every type of discrimination, whether social or cultural, whether based on sex, race, color, social condition, language, or religion is to be overcome and eradicated as contrary to God's intent" (*Gaudium et Spes*). Good ministry looks toward the Kingdom of God as its measure for the society's common good.

The good that is held in common for Christians, of course, is Christ. And it is finally in the celebration of Christ's cross and resurrection that we come to see and understand the Church's common good. Good ministry leads the community—the weak and strong, the innocent and guilty—to dare to stand in solidarity at the foot of cross proclaiming God's amazing gift of loving friendship and redemption to all the world.

FOR REFLECTION

1. When we look into the eyes of each person, do we see the *imago Dei*? Do we treat each person with respect and dignity as a child of God?

2. In what ways do we invite people into full participation in our community of faith?

3. Where do we hear the cry of the poor today? Is there poverty in our midst that requires prophetic witness and pastoral accompaniment?

4. In what ways do we stand at the foot of the cross and accompany those who suffer?

5. How do we walk with those who are guilty and seek God's mercy?

6. How do we recognize God's gifts in each person? How do we help others in recognizing their vocation? How do we invite their gifts and charisms to be shared in community?

7. How are we empowering the domestic and local church to be the Body of Christ in the home and neighborhood?

8. In what ways are we a light for the world? How are we reaching beyond our local concerns to see and understand the larger society and world? Where can we, as a local community, serve the common good of God's people?

12. CENTERED IN GOD

Roberta C. Bondi*

What is it that makes a truly good minister? Considering the great variety of people who go into ministry, and the even greater variety to be found in our congregations around this country, of course it is hard to come up with a short list of the qualities we would hope for in every person in ministry. Even a partial list would have to include a love of God and a love of the people of God, an active intelligence, sociological and psychological knowledge of the state of the church in general and the congregation she or he is serving in particular, a willingness to take the world seriously and with love. Then there are skills in both spiritual direction and counseling, an inclusive vision with respect to gender, race, age, and nationality, a working knowledge of scripture, the Christian tradition, and the modern theological resources that are available, and a certain kind of gregariousness. On top of all these, we would want to find a strong but not legalistic ethical orientation, knowledge of how to deal with a plumbing or rodent crisis, skills in preaching and leading good worship, a sense of responsibility, organizational skills, a commitment to the mission of the church, an ability to lead and a style of leadership that respects the congregation, energy, a certain kind of savvy with respect to money, political sensitivity, and an ability see when it is necessary to draw on outside help and to know where to get it.

Needless to say, it is obvious that this is a lot (!) to expect of the average minister, and to prepare a person in all these ways for ministry is a lot to expect from ourselves as well. At the same time, I suspect that there is very little here, with the exception, perhaps, of pest control and plumbing, that any of us would really want to relegate to second place importance, much less leave out of our list entirely. So what do we, as educators for real ministry in vital congregations do with all this? Is there any single logical place to start thinking about this? Any center out of which all the rest comes?

The early monastic material I teach and upon which I do research, my experience of twenty-four years of seminary teaching and going around the country leading workshops and retreats in various protestant, Roman Catholic, and even Orthodox settings, both liberal and conservative, and my own most intimate struggle with the Christian life tells me that, in fact, there is one single center out of which all good ministry flows, a single foundation which makes its learning, and its teaching, possible. That center and foundation is a deep grounding in God through prayer and self-reflection that allows the minister to find and know that her or his most basic identity and deepest and most concrete security lie in God, and only in God, and not in success, or in pleasing someone else, or in being seen as a good person, or being loved by a congregation (or a class of students), or in being "successful."

Let me draw on my own non-teaching but painfully relevant experience to try to illustrate for you what I mean by this finding identity in God. Fifteen years ago when our daughter started college she begged us to buy her a car. For a number of reasons, both financial and related to what was going on in her chaotic life, this was clearly a very bad idea. After two or three months of serious hassling, however, she took matters into her own hands and bought herself a motor scooter. Needless to say, I was terrified as well as angry. When I told her I was worried she would kill or maim herself on it, she responded that, if I were a good mother and really loved her, I would have bought her the car. Further pleading, explaining, and arguing over the next year were unsuccessful. Her charges of lack of love and bad motherhood continued, and during the months that followed she traded in the scooter for three more, ever-larger motorcycles.

My frustration, fear, and sense of failure were unlimited during this time, and my daily prayers were ever the same: "Please, please, God. I just want to be a good mother. Help me to see what I need to sacrifice in order to love my daughter enough that she gets rid of the motorcycle and doesn't kill herself." My prayer was not answered in any obvious way, however, and eventually I fell into despair.

* Roberta Bondi is Professor of Church History, Candler School of Theology, Emory University, Atlanta, Ga.

Exhausted, one morning I simply gave up. Sitting in my chair in the presence of God, I had no more will to ask for help in being a good mother, no will even to try to love. I could see what was going wrong, and I hardly even cared. Then, in this despairing state of prayer, I heard these familiar and gracious words from the Fifth Century Sayings of the Desert Fathers repeating in my head: "Abba Alonius used to say, 'Unless a person say in her heart, in the world there is no one but myself and God, that person will not find peace..'"

"No one but myself and God!" All at once I understood for the first time what the ancient desert father was trying to teach me, and at the very same instant I saw what it was I had been doing and what I was lacking. More than anything in the world I had longed to be a good mother. I had needed to be "a good mother," but being a good mother was about how I saw myself, not about my daughter—and without thought I had given to her the job of deciding whether or not I was. Of course, the whole attempt was doomed to failure in every respect, for as long as I could not find access in myself to the fact that it is only God who created me, sustained me, utterly accepts me, and bestows my value on me, and not my daughter or any other human being, I could not find the peace that was, in fact, necessary to love her in the very way she needed. I couldn't even *see* what she needed, couldn't see *her* because the whole business at my end was about my self-reflexive need to "be a good mother." Understanding this in that moment in prayer I finally took in the fact that she was no longer a child, and I saw what she really did need. I resolved, therefore, neither to mention the motorcycle again nor to allow myself to fall into the "good mother" trap. Three weeks later without further discussion she sold the motorcycle. My new certainty that I do not have to earn from any human being the right to breathe the air because it is already given to me by God did not resolve all her problems, but she didn't kill herself or anybody else.

This is a long example but, I believe, an important one for thinking through the analogous issues around good ministry in real congregations. "What is the greatest commandment?" Jesus was asked, and his answer was unequivocal: "You shall love the Lord your God and your neighbor as yourself." Love of God and neighbor is the goal of the Christian life, and if ministers are not able to do the first, first, or confuse the first with the second, disaster is sure to

follow. They will use love, not for the sake of the people entrusted to them, but for their own unconscious or conscious ends. If this is true of mothers, it is most certainly true of ministers.

Unless they can find that center in God, they will never be competent ministers and their congregations will pay for it. Unconsciously or consciously, they will do the things in their churches that they think they need to affirm their being and give them value in their own eyes, and they will not do the things that threaten that value given by others. They may not be able to tell the difference between the structures and pronouncements of the church and the God they profess to serve. They may be authoritarian, inauthentic, threatened not only by new social patterns, but also by new theological approaches, dismissive of the Christian tradition, or rigid with respect to it. They may be wishy-washy, disdainful, lazy, self-deceptive, sexually predatory, financially crooked, self-protective, bitter or resentful, passive-aggressive, controlling, defensive, unable to set priorities, and/or ultimately, burned out.

On the other hand, if they are sure in the depths of their being that their center rests in God, and they know how to keep in constant awareness of it, those same ministers can truly grow into the right kind of love of the people they serve. They will not be afraid of the elderly, the sick, the handicapped, or the dying, and they will insist on a place for them in their congregations. They will care about the poor. They will see folks as they really are and not be judgmental because they will be very sure that God loves all of the congregation infinitely, as God loves the ministers themselves, and they will communicate that love convincingly. They will be anxious to drink deeply of our common Christian resources in scripture, tradition, and modern theology, and they will be hungry to find ways to share with their congregations in the clearest possible manner the practical, saving insights of those resources. They will not be personally threatened by changes in the world around them, such as the women's movement or an influx of non-English-speaking parishioners, that affect them and their congregation, because they know that their stability is in God, who is ever faithful.

They will draw on whatever resources they need to do their jobs without feeling ashamed that they are limited, because we are all limited. They will be courageous about speaking the truth, risking new ventures, doing things differently, preaching the word, not because it makes them feel good, but because they want to help their congregations. They will love the world God created with their whole hearts and encourage their congregations to the same love. And if they are told, as one of our students was a few years ago when he went before his board of ministry to request an inner-city church, that "no one ever got to a tall steeple church by starting out in the slums," they will only laugh.

If this is true of ministry, then, I believe that the starting point for all education for ministry is Christian formation that helps the student learn the long-term ways of prayer and self-reflection that will sustain her or him through seminary and through all the years of ministry which will follow it. Such formation should focus on working with the student in such a way that he or she is taught not only how to acquire facts, but how to bring his or her deepest, and perhaps hardest-to-find self into conversation with those facts, of scriptural studies, or church history, or sociology of religion, or ethics, or pastoral care, in the presence of the Trinitarian God of love for the transformation and healing of that self which is going into ministry.

I am excruciatingly aware that this is not an easy task to set ourselves. Few of us were actually trained to do it (I certainly wasn't), and many of us were explicitly trained not to do it. Further, it is hard, labor-intensive work, and so also very expensive. Not many of my students, at least, come with anything like a regular practice of prayer, unless they are very conservative, and in addition few of my students come with more than a sketchy sense of the contents of the Christian tradition, much less with a knowledge of why it is existentially important, say, that we insist on the equality of the persons in the Trinity or that when we look at Jesus we see God as surely as we see a human being. Many come to us suspecting that we want to take away their faith, and so distrust education.

These are enormous problems, to be sure, and they won't be solved just by hiring a few more people or fiddling a bit with the curriculum. Still, I believe our churches are in a major crisis. If we are truly to train ministers to minister effectively to real congregations in the years ahead of us, then we simply must make Christian formation in prayer and reflection, and formation for ministry, the starting point, as well as the end point, of theological education.

FOR REFLECTION

1. What do you identify as the positive spiritual qualities of a minister that are crucial for ministry?

2. Do you believe these can, in some sense, be taught and learned in seminary?

3. What practical tools are available to you for such teaching if you believe it possible? How would you set about doing it?

4. Is it important that they be taught throughout the curriculum or is there a certain appropriate place such teaching belongs? Are they integral enough to the program that students understand that developing them is a fundamental part of their school work?

5. What do you do with students who really do seem to lack these qualities and resources when they reach the end of their course work? Graduate them anyway? Warn them that they will do harm to themselves and others in ministry unless they find a way to address them?

13. GOOD PASTORAL LEADERSHIP FOR THE 21ST CENTURY

Jackson W. Carroll*

In an article in the *Boston Sunday Globe*, the writer Paul Wilkes reflected on visits to Protestant and Catholic churches across the nation. He concluded that "in too many of our parishes, we have [clergy] who are sadly ordinary, . . .who had they ended up in any other field would be seen as second-rate practitioners." Although Wilkes is correct in his judgment about the ordinariness demonstrated by many clergy, we all know others who exhibit extraordinary leadership abilities. What makes the difference? Do extraordinary pastoral leaders possess innate qualities and gifts that "sadly ordinary" clergy lack? If so, theological schools can do little but be midwives, bringing to birth what is already present innately–and pray that those other students who lack the necessary innate gifts don't do too much harm. But if good leaders are not born but are in some respects "made," then there is an important role for theological educators and other mentors.

To be sure there are "gifts and graces" that contribute to good leadership. Some are probably innate; others are the products of one's upbringing and the opportunities that one's prior experiences have offered. Nonetheless, I want to argue that there are attributes of good pastoral leadership that can be described and acquired through education, mentoring, and discipline. I prefer to use the word "good" rather than "excellent" to describe pastoral leadership, because "excellence" has been used so widely and loosely in managerial literature in recent years that its meaning has been diminished.

My title refers to good pastoral leadership *for the 21st century* or at least for these early years of the new century. This is a way of saying that good pastoral leadership must be understood contextually. Partly this means taking into account the way that various ecclesial traditions have differing understandings and expectations for pastoral leadership. Similarly, various congregational types and contexts–small, mid-sized, or large; urban, suburban, or rural– often require different styles of leadership. Especially, however, I want to emphasize that the current social and cultural context places its own unique demands on pastoral leadership that cannot be ignored regardless of ecclesial tradition or congregational type. Obviously the events of September 11, 2001, and their aftermath reflect a major new contextual reality–our vulnerability as a nation to global terrorism. But prior to those terrible events we have already experienced the unparalleled growth of religious pluralism in the United States and an increasing privatization of religious life. We have also seen the expansion of special purpose groups that advocate for this or that social or theological position and make battlegrounds of congregations and denominations. Moreover, a consumer culture afflicts congregational life and leadership as individuals pick and choose among various religious alternatives in the process of self-authoring their religious identities. These alternatives are not only offered by different congregations or religious traditions but by a virtual spirituality industry of self-help books, gurus, and groups that have moved onto the turf once held by more traditionally defined pastoral leaders. And finally, there is the rapidity of change, what someone has called a "white water world," that poses constant adaptive challenges to all institutions including the church. Such contextual challenges must be held in view as the backdrop against which good pastoral leadership is exercised, and they make pastoral leadership all the more important.

To put it as succinctly as possible, I understand good pastoral leadership to be the process of helping a congregation embody in its corporate life the practices that shape vital Christian life and community in ways that are faithful to the Gospel and appropriate to the particular congregation's size, resources, and setting–especially its existence in 21st century American society. In this sense, the process of leading a congregation is itself a constitutive practice. What, more specifically, does this involve? It can be broken further in at least the following tasks:

- teaching a congregation about the meaning of practices that shape vital and faithful Christian life and community–that is, an interpretive task;

- helping a congregation gain a critical understanding of its current practices, resources–that is, a resource mobilization task;

* Jackson Carroll is Director of Pulpit & Pew: Research on Pastoral Leadership and Williams Professor Emeritus of Religion and Society, Duke University Divinity School, Durham, N.C.

- helping a congregation gain a vision of itself as a vital Christian community that is realistic given its size and resources and setting—that is, an envisioning task;

- motivating a congregation's members to pursue its vision by shaping its practices in keeping with the vision—that is, a motivational and "incarnational" task;

- helping the congregation find the resources—spiritual, intellectual, and material—to pursue the vision and maintain its life—that is, a resource development task;

- coping with and managing the inevitable conflicts that come from multiple constituencies and points of view in the congregation—that is, a political task;

- monitoring the congregation's life and practices so that they retain their faithfulness to the Gospel in light of ever-changing reality—that is, a task of ongoing renewal.

Such reflexivity requires pastoral leaders who are not only grounded in the traditions of faith and traditional arts of ministry, but who have lively imaginations and the capacity for thinking "outside the box."

These tasks will be carried out differently in different congregations, taking into account the congregation's denominational tradition, history, size and context; but taken together, they constitute the practice of good pastoral leadership.

I have cast the tasks in terms of the responsibility of the pastoral leader; yet, it is obvious that they are not ones that a single pastoral leader can do alone. Instead they constitute a set of *shared responsibilities* that involve the cooperation and collaboration of pastoral leaders, lay leaders, and members. The pastoral leader is the one who will typically take primary responsibility for seeing that the various tasks get done, but she or he cannot practice leadership alone. It is a shared responsibility—the work of the congregation as a whole. This is the clear message of Paul's metaphor of the body of Christ with the various constituent members working together to build up the whole body in Christ.

Because the pastoral leader has a special responsibility in the overall practice of leadership in Christian communities and because, as theological educators, we are in the business of educating pastoral leaders, I want to suggest two attributes that are not innate that I believe are essential and that we have some responsibility for shaping.

First, there is the matter of *competence* in the pastoral tasks, both traditional and more recent, that define the pastoral role. Traditionally and typically we have understood these competencies to include solid grounding in knowledge of the Bible and the historical traditions of the church as well as skill in the various arts of ministry. These traditional pastoral tasks obviously continue to be important, and they are vehicles through which many of the leadership tasks that I described are exercised. Pastors still spend most of their time presiding at worship, preaching, teaching, giving pastoral care, and administering the work of the congregation. Good pastoral leaders value the goods that these activities produce, and they are motivated to spend the time and energy necessary to do them well. They are willing to accept the spiritual and intellectual disciplines that the doing the tasks well demand. Someone has referred to this hard work as reflecting the "mundanity" of excellence.

But in addition to these more traditional pastoral competencies, leadership in the current social and cultural context calls for another competence not always included in seminary education: the capacity for reflexivity, or what elsewhere I have called reflective leadership. Reflexivity involves neither an unyielding obeisance to one's tradition nor an unthinking, "knee jerk" response to the cultural changes taking place about us. Instead, it entails a deliberative response not unlike Aristotle's "practical wisdom" or *phronesis*—a wisdom that involves holding in creative tension the goods of the tradition *and* the challenges of the present situation, so that one informs the other in an ongoing dialogue or argument. In this reflexive process, the tradition remains a living one as it is retraditioned in the encounter with the present. In the same process, one's response to the present avoids simple accommodation but rather is an adaptation of congregational practices informed and guided by the argument with the tradition. Such reflexivity requires pastoral leaders who are not only grounded in the traditions of faith and traditional arts of ministry, but who have lively imaginations and the capacity for thinking "outside the box."

One further word about competence. Typically, seminary teaching about the pastoral role has been done from a pastor-centered or clerical paradigm of leadership. These tasks are what pastors do to and for laity, as if the pastor—the "shepherd"—is the central actor in the church's life and laity—the "sheep"—are essentially passive recipients. What is needed instead, to elaborate my earlier point about shared leadership, is a shift to an ecclesial paradigm so that competent, reflexive engagement in pastoral tasks become part of the practice of *congregational* leadership, ways that congregations are helped to become vital Christian communities. In a recent book on the changing face of the Catholic priesthood, Donald Cozens describes this shift with reference to the role of the post-Vatican II priest. The role of the priest, he says, (and Protestants can mostly substitute pastor for priest) has shifted from a cultic model to one of servant leadership in a community; from being on a pedestal to participation as a leader-companion with his people; from being a preacher teaching the truths of the faith and morally correct behavior to one who bears the mystery of God and leads the people into a more intimate contact with that mystery; from a lone ranger with unique sacramental powers to a collaborative ministry that focuses on the gifts of the parish as a whole; from a monastic spirituality that sets the priest apart from the people to a secular spirituality that is nourished by the rhythms of parish life; from saving souls from the world to liberating God's people to live fully in the world. Such a shift of models has not been easy for older priests who were formed in the cultic model of ministry, or for lay Catholics raised in a pre-Vatican II church. Nor is the shift from a clerical to an ecclesial paradigm an easy one for Protestants to make, whether in reshaping theological education or reorienting the practices of pastors, congregations, and denominations. Yet, I believe that this paradigm shift is absolutely essential if the church today is going to be able to meet the challenges of the post-traditional, post-Christian context in which we live. And it is essential in shaping the competence of good pastoral leaders.

But competence alone is insufficient. *Character grounded in one's sense of calling* is also an essential attribute of the good leader. The pastoral leader not only *does* something in and for the church. She or he also *is* something—a symbol of God's presence and purposes. Although different ecclesial traditions would express it differently, pastoral leaders are bearers of God's mystery as first among equals in a priestly community that itself is also called to bear God's mystery in the world. This is to say that good pastoral leaders not only do things competently, but in exercising leadership they also exhibit what John Fletcher has called "religious authenticity." They have "head and heart together." Without such authenticity, it is unlikely that leaders will be able to establish the necessary fiduciary bond that makes it possible for them to lead and for laity to trust their leadership. This is especially true when congregational members have to make difficult decisions personally or corporately, when changing circumstances challenge old and well-loved ways of

doing things and make change and adaptation imperative. Such adaptive challenges require that pastoral leaders not only exercise authority based on their competence, but also personal authority based on their character, rooted in a lively sense of call. It is personal authority that makes it possible for leaders to establish what some have called a "holding environment," a relationship that enables a pastoral leader to give back the work of ministry to the people, helping them make hard but necessary decisions, and holding each other accountable for faithful Christian living.

The good pastoral leader's character is, in last analysis, not self-generated, but it is grounded in one's relationship to God, in one's call to ministry. The call is not only a "churchly" call—an acknowledgment by a congregation or denomination that one has the requisite gifts, graces, and competence to lead—but it is a "secret" call that signifies a deep and abiding relationship with God. Such a relationship is nurtured and sustained through regularly engaging in the hard work of spiritual discipline, even as pastoral competence is nurtured and enlarged in the hard work of intellectual discipline.

Character devoid of competence will be ineffective in face of the challenges of pastoral leadership in today's world. But without character nurtured in one's relationship with God, one's competence will have roots too shallow to motivate, sustain, and enliven good pastoral leadership.

FOR REFLECTION

1. The author provides one perspective on the theme of "Good Ministry." What needs to be added? How are competence and character related? Do you agree with the author's emphasis on the two?

2. What factors or forces hinder good ministry from happening today?

3. What resources (spiritual, intellectual, interpersonal, economic, etc.) are needed to sustain good ministry? Are they being adequately provided? By whom?

4. What role does theological education have to play in nurturing and sustaining good ministry? What role do denominations play? Local congregations? Clergy themselves?

5. What will need to be changed in our current way of doing things (as theological schools, denominations, congregations, clergy) if we are to nurture and sustain good ministry?

14. Virtues, Dispositions, and Practices

Christine D. Pohl[*]

My initial reaction to an invitation to reflect on good ministry is to think, "Somehow, you know it when you see it, when you're part of it." Even under the most difficult circumstances, when ministry is good, you sense that you are catching a glimpse of the Kingdom. Nevertheless, it is possible to identify some common commitments, virtues, dispositions, and practices that combine to make ministry good, even when the contexts, circumstances, resources, and personalities differ widely.

Shaped by a sustaining awareness of God's love, good ministry involves ongoing responses characterized by gratitude, dependence, and delight. Communities whose ministry is good are made up of persons who are individually and corporately grateful for the goodness and love they find in God and in the people around them. They are prayerful communities that understand the importance of their labor and its ambiguity, knowing that unless God "builds the house, those who build it labor in vain." Such communities faithfully fulfill the tasks of ministry while also realizing that they are dependent on God as the source of their life and hope. Good ministry, then, recognizes the marvelous and peculiar relation between divine grace and human effort, God's provision and our responsibility.

Christians who practice good ministry delight in God, in the wonder of the Trinity, and in the mystery of grace. At the center of good ministry is Jesus, through whose life, death, and resurrection we find life, reconciliation, and holiness. In good ministry, the love we have seen and experienced in God and within the community of faith turns outward in practices of love and reconciliation with neighbor, stranger, and enemy. In particular, our orientation is turned toward those with whom Jesus most closely identified, those the larger community often dismisses and overlooks.

Good ministry is an embodied reflection and expression of the welcome we have found in Christ.

In ministry that is good, participants recognize the close and crucial connections between what we do and say in our gatherings for worship and in our daily practices. Worship as corporate response to God's acts and character can spill into every practice and transform it, whether that practice is teaching, hospitality, child-rearing, or burying the dead. And, for the Christian, practices find their deepest meaning in worship.[1]

Good ministry requires an on-going attentiveness to pastoral and community formation, both moral and spiritual. It involves faithfulness and forgiveness in small and large matters. While dependent on the integrity and trustworthiness of participants and their steady commitment to personal and corporate holiness, good ministry can absorb failure and frailty without being shattered.

Those engaged in good ministry recognize the close relationship between goals and the means by which they are pursued. Quite frequently, committed seminarians and pastors sincerely proclaim that they will do "whatever it takes…to build the church…to see that justice is done…to proclaim the good news…to work for the Kingdom." Although such commitment is commendable, this approach to ministry increases the risk that Christians will overlook the moral and spiritual significance of means and strategies and, as a result, miss the goals they are seeking. As Martin Luther King Jr. wrote in "Pilgrimage to Nonviolence," "the end is preexistent in the mean[s]."[2] The temptation to use and justify moral shortcuts for the sake of the Kingdom takes many forms, but it is strong in our pragmatically-oriented culture. An approach to ministry bounded only by "whatever it takes" invites moral and spiritual disaster; good ministry views means and ends as inseparable.

The following five dyads identify dimensions of Christian practice and commitment that are understood best in relation to one another. They are not

---

* Christine Pohl is Professor of Social Ethics, Asbury Theological Seminary, Wilmore, Ky.

[1] See Craig Dykstra and Dorothy C. Bass, "A Theological Understanding of Christian Practices," in *Practicing Theology*, ed. Miroslav Volf and Dorothy C. Bass (Grand Rapids: Wm. B. Eerdmans, 2002), 13-32.

[2] Martin Luther King Jr., "Pilgrimage to Nonviolence," in *Stride Toward Freedom* (New York: Harper & Row, 1958, 1986), 92.

exactly paradoxes, though there is substantial tension in trying to hold each pair together; the tension is part of what makes good ministry distinctive.

Hospitality and a Clear Sense of Identity/Boundaries: Hospitality is central to good ministry because it is basic to who we are as followers of Jesus. "Welcome," writes Jean Vanier, "is one of the signs that a community is alive." Inviting others into our lives and communities "is a sign that…we have a treasure of truth and of peace to share."[3] Whatever the context for good ministry, it involves a welcoming community that is rich with stories, rituals, history, and covenantal bonds of faithfulness and responsibility.

But to be able to offer strangers a place that is rich with meanings and relationships, a community needs boundaries and commitments that preserve its identity and values. The practice of hospitality challenges the boundaries of a community while it simultaneously depends on that community's identity to make a space that nourishes life. While hospitality depends on defined communities, it always presses those communities outward to make the circle of care larger. Thus, hospitality and good ministry require the crossing of significant social boundaries and a simultaneous affirmation of certain distinctions. Discerning the particular characteristics of a fruitful relationship between distinctive identity and a consistent, non-coercive welcome of strangers is a key dimension of good ministry.[4]

Awareness of Vulnerability and Cultivation of Excellence: Those involved in good ministry yearn to be good, to grow in faithfulness, grace, and purpose, and to give our best to God and neighbor. Good ministry is an expression of excellence that grows as we cultivate virtue, vision, and skill. But good ministry also involves a recognition of, and truthfulness about, our own vulnerability, inadequacy, and sin. Although it can be difficult to be honest about personal vulnerabilities in ministry, hiding them yields ministry that is dishonest and dangerous.

We tend to equate excellence with sustained personal effort, but for the Christian excellence is also connected with dependence on God's strength. While recognizing the importance of skill and competence in ministry, we need also to acknowledge the normative place of weakness in the New Testament. Paul assures us that in weakness we see the power of God most clearly.[5] Good ministry affirms the mysterious connection between the cross and our healing, among brokenness, holiness, and wholeness.

Attentiveness to the Moment and Bold Cultivation of a Larger Vision: When engaged in good ministry, we are held by a vision of God and God's reign that keeps us from getting lost in the details of daily maintenance, from getting caught in life-draining projects that are no bigger than our own immediate interests. Because of confidence in God's generous purposes, followers of Jesus can take risks and minister without besetting fears; faithful Christians can live out a vision for transformation, justice, and peace. Sustained by grace, we can focus less on control, management, and measurable results, and more on modeling and mentoring lives that are lived in response to grace. When our security is located in God, we can deal with the unpredictability of seeking righteousness and can more readily give generously of our resources and ourselves.

This vision of God and God's good purposes must be held together with the importance of attending to the moment. We sometimes mistake frenzied engagement with detail for attentiveness. But disciplined attentiveness involves being fully present to the persons with and to whom we minister and to the events of our day. A disposition and practice of attentiveness is appreciative of each person's individuality, needs, stories, and gifts. Such attentiveness involves tenacity that does not give up in the face of trouble, that willingly accompanies persons when their problems cannot be "fixed," and that understands sacrifice within a larger picture that is life-affirming.

Individual Responsibility and Commitment to Community: Good ministry is deeply communal, attentive to mutual strengthening within the whole community. It is less focused on exceptionally gifted individuals and is more the result of a community that recognizes and values each person's contributions and bears each one's burdens.[6] Good ministry requires a continual interaction between this commitment to community and a seriousness about individual responsibility and maturity.

---

[3]   Jean Vanier, *Community and Growth,* rev. ed. (New York: Paulist, 1989), 266-7.

[4]   For further discussion on this topic, see Christine D. Pohl, *Making Room: Recovering Hospitality as a Christian Tradition* (Grand Rapids: Wm. B. Eerdmans, 1999), 135-41.

[5]   See, for example, 1 Corinthians 1:18-2:5; 2 Corinthians 12:8-10.

[6]   1 Corinthians 12; Galatians 6:2.

While good ministry is more about faithful communities than about religious superstars, it does require individuals who are growing in holiness. Communities can assist the process or undermine it. Through support and accountability, people grow toward maturity. But when communities allow weakness to be an excuse for stagnation, self-indulgence, and carelessness, they find individual growth and goodness threatening. In those circumstances, communities can undermine personal and corporate yearnings for Christlikeness. In good ministry, participants recognize that individual and communal wholeness and holiness are for the sake of the world.

Rootedness in the Tradition and Sympathetic Engagement with Contemporary Culture: Good ministry is rooted and renewed in Scripture and finds the historic Christian tradition to be a rich resource for contemporary life and worship. But this appreciation for the tradition can become elitist nostalgia if not accompanied by deep love for the people of today.

Good ministry takes seriously the questions that people are asking and responds to the deep yearnings of this generation. It requires that we identify fruitful points of contact between Christian faith and contemporary culture and places of grave divergence. For this we need to be able to read and exegete cultures and communities with the same seriousness that we exegete Scripture and attend to historic texts. Good ministry, then, is able to discern the particular ways in which the Gospel is life-giving news for our time.

FOR REFLECTION

1. How might churches cultivate a culture of gratitude?

2. In what ways can we encourage a closer connection between worship and other practices (e.g. hospitality to strangers, sabbath-keeping, caring for the body, or child-rearing)?

3. What parts of your particular congregational identity and tradition are helpful in welcoming strangers and what parts make offering welcome more difficult?

4. How does truthfulness about vulnerability and personal inadequacy contribute to good ministry?

5. How can congregations and their pastors hold together a big vision for ministry with attentiveness to particular individuals and their needs?